1982

Instant Parent

Instant Parent

A Guide for Stepparents,
Part-Time Parents
and Grandparents

by Suzy Kalter

Introduction by
Howard A. Britton, M.D.

A & W PUBLISHERS, INC.
New York

The names of my husband's first wife and their daughter have been changed to protect their privacy.

His and her, mother and father are used interchangeably. If a topic applies only to one sex, it is so stated.

Published by
A & W Publishers, Inc.
95 Madison Avenue
New York, New York 10016

Library of Congress Cataloging in Publication Data

Kalter, Suzy.
  Instant parent.

  1. Parenting—United States.   2. Stepparents—United
States.   3. Grandparents—United States.
I. Title.
HQ755.8.K34   301.42'7   79-14904
ISBN 0-89479-030-7
Printed in the United States of America

For Aggie and Dixie
and my sweet Mick

Contents

Preface

I have interviewed a president of the United States, stood before the board of directors of a Fortune 500 Company and given an hour-long presentation, and even eaten dinner alone in some of the country's fanciest restaurants, but the hardest thing I have ever done in my life was to become a stepmother. I have never been a real-live mother, but I know that it's easier than being a part-time mother to someone else's children.

We can all pretty much choose whether or not we want to become parents. We can't say as much for becoming stepparents. It comes with the "for-better-or-for-worse" marriage vow. Yes, of course I knew I was marrying a man with a child from a previous marriage. He didn't try to hide her or deceive me into thinking she wouldn't be important; I was just very unprepared for what it meant. I kept saying things like, "Gee, I just love little girls" and "What size does she wear?" I had absolutely no idea of what was ahead of me.

Yet before I even had the gold band on my hand and the thank-you notes to write, I became a mother. Worse: a full-time part-time mother. That is to say, his daughter arrived to live with us for one month. She was seven years old and her own mother was three-thousand miles away. She was frightened, so I jumped in not only to help her, but also to make us all a family. On her second day with us I bought her the most beautiful gingham and white eyelet diary in the world to keep a record of her month with us. That's when I found out she could barely write. She couldn't tell time and wasn't terrific at tying her own shoelaces, either. She wasn't much better at dressing herself and couldn't read with any ease. She was not an independent little person to share my days with, but rather a lost kid who needed constant care and supervision. It was a total shock to me.

In the next month I learned to rearrange my schedule

to include my job, my husband, and a seven-year-old child. I found out how to make a school lunch, how to find a baby-sitter, and how to express my anger at being put in such a ridiculous position (motherhood) without any training. The more I learned, the more I saw that there was to learn. I discovered I was completely trained to function in a business world but knew nothing about a mother's world. I found little information in libraries that could help me. The only available books on stepparenting were filled with horror stories, tales of nervous breakdowns and complex psychological dramas. I've tried to leave those out of this book and provide, instead, the how-to information I so desperately needed.

—Suzy Kalter
Hollywood, California

Acknowledgments

This book would never have been written (or necessary) without my husband, who held my hand throughout, even while I was trying to type. All my thanks to him. Many thanks also to my research assistant, Susan Belmonte; my editor, Angela Miller; my eye doctor, Dr. William Fein; and Dr. Howard Britton. Also, many thanks to my Susans.

I am also most appreciative of the hundreds of children who filled out questionnaires and the stepparents who answered even my most personal questions.

Introduction

In this age of instant coffee, instant soup, and instant money, it's only to be expected that instant parenting would also evolve. As remarkable as it may seem, you may now have, or become, any of these things in a matter of seconds. The soup and the coffee just need water. The money, alas, requires credit. And the parent part comes quite quickly if you marry a person with children from a previous marriage. When a formerly single, childless adult marries a formerly married parent, there you have it, voilà: instant parent.

But not a parent without instant problems. There is no substitute for a planned pregnancy, nine months of gestation, the pains and joys of childbearing, and several months of breast-feeding. Yet, increasingly, as the divorce rate rises, we have more and more American adults achieving parenthood without any of the aforementioned. As a result, they experience a set of problems unique to their new situation.

While most instant parents enter into their new role with positive, even enthusiastic, feelings, they are totally—emotionally and educationally—unprepared for what lies ahead. A person who has never been a parent cannot overnight become a parent and expect to live happily ever after.

A divorce and a remarriage are difficult rites of passage for all participants, the formerly married and the children. When another person, from outside the original family, enters the group and claims equal rights of membership, a new crisis ensues. The drama affects each member of the new marriage, as well as the children and the former spouse. A stranger with little experience in child rearing suddenly becomes the focal point of the family, the target of curiosity and animosity.

Suzy Kalter has written the first book created specifically for adults who suddenly find themselves instant parents or grandparents. Finally there is a text available delineating the feelings and foibles of instant parents. From how to make cinnamon toast to how to keep from competing with a former spouse, Ms. Kalter humorously identifies the problems of a new breed of parent and then outlines a practical and workable solution.

Her book can be read from cover to cover as a treatise on the life of a stepparent, or used as I prescribe it, in doses, for quick and proper reference. The three reference chapters in the book have been prepared with meticulous care and are fully corroborated by myself as medically and age-appropriately correct. For the person with no former experience with children, all one needs is the index or table of contents of *Instant Parent* to procure the desired information, be it how-to, hand holding, or notes on the joys and sorrows of stepparenting. For the dating single, *Instant Parent's* reference chapters alone provide a compendium of information that will help start anyone in a promising relationship with someone else's children.

Although the libraries and bookstores are crammed with volumes covering every aspect of child raising, *Instant Parent* is one of the few books that gives a wide breadth of pertinent information in an easily digestible form. One need not juggle six or seven other books or consult several experts when a quick look inside *Instant Parent* will probably suffice.

I recommend *Instant Parent* to any man or woman who suddenly finds himself in a child-caring position, for an hour, a day, or a lifetime. You will find this book of immeasurable value and, next to chicken soup, your greatest ally.

—Howard A. Britton, M.D.

1.
Who Are These Children?

I Always Wanted to be a Mommy

I always knew I wanted to be a mommy. It was the true and honest goal of every young girl born of the postwar baby boom. Adults bent down on folded knees, squatting into childlike heights, and asked what you wanted to be when you grew up. It was a ritual.

"I want to be a Mommy," was the only acceptable answer for a little girl.

I remember the day my aspiration moved toward reality as I crossed that hazy border between subconscious acceptance of the command *Thou Shalt Mother* and the clear knowledge that any woman can.

I was about six. And lying on the daybed (yes, in those days we still had daybeds) in the makeshift den (we weren't rich enough to have a real den). I was home from school with some childhood disease and was only sick enough to demand to be propped up on the daybed with a lot of pillows and mother's bed jacket, the satin one with the pink rosebuds.

Mother was largely pregnant with my sister, so babies were obviously on the mind. As mother waddled around the apartment, I occupied myself with my favorite game: that old standby Let's Have Babies, brought to you by Mother Nature and sponsored by every home in America.

Coyly, I would place my rubber infant (this was before Betsy Wetsy) under the covers atop my stomach, simulating pregnancy as best I could, then pop, throw the doll up from stomach to ceiling with both arms. This game progressed all afternoon as baby after baby was conceived and delivered without any help from anyone else. (I was a very independent child.)

The babies would be named appropriately with a high ratio of girls names because I liked girls' names better. They weren't all girls however, because even at six I knew the law of averages was against me. After all, God had already sent me a baby brother two years ago, so I knew the world was one of wicked chance.

The imaginary babies were born (*pop*), tucked under the covers next to my face on the pillow, cooed to for the proper length of time, and then ignored with the arrival of each sibling.

Motherhood and I stayed in close touch over the years.

When I wasn't dominating my doll, or giving orders to my newborn sister, I liked to dress up the cat, Smokey, in baby clothes and pretend she was my baby. I relocated my sister so I had undisputed use of the baby carriage, and then replaced Debbie with Smokey and toured the neighborhood as if she were an infant. The cat, of course, had a mind of her own: she often jumped out of the pram—baby bunting and all—and ran under the house, the only place she was safe from my too-tight-across-the-belly grasp.

But then, she was just a cat and I was a little girl. I finally outsmarted her by tying her *into* the baby carriage. Mercifully, my parents spoke out on the need for cats to be treated like cats. So much for Smokey and her role as Cat Baby.

Finally, my sister grew up to be old enough to be my slave. Ah, blessed day. She did whatever I told her. We played house a lot. I was mother (of course) and she was baby (why not?). We did once modify the game so that I was mother and she was a pet tiger, but my parents didn't like that very much and stopped it.

By the time I entered junior high school, it was no longer "in" to play dolls or dream about being a mommy. The only important thing in life was being a cheerleader—everyone knew that. Already Ellie Nelson had become pregnant and disappeared from our lives. She was soon followed by others who were always getting mononucleosis and then moving to Washington or changing schools. Obviously you could take this motherhood thing just too far.

As I reached the end of my college career, it became obvious that I was not about to be a mother. First of all, I took biology instead of botany. That may mean little to you, but I found a direct correlation with the number of unwanted pregnancies among my friends and the students who chose stems over sternums. And then, too, I never did meet Mr. Right. I never did get dropped, pinned, engaged, married, and pregnant the way the legend said I should.

So I made a lot of hurried plans for an elaborate career, created my own hope chest (hope-I-live-in-a-brown-stone) and moved off to New York, telling everyone I had more on my mind than marriage and maternity. I was full of bull, but I was cornered.

I finally met Mr. Right some seven years later. And although he was, and is, very much my Mr. Right, there was a small matter no one had ever mentioned before—he was also someone's Daddy.

As easily as I had laid on a daybed some twenty-two years earlier, once again—just when I'd given up believing in instant anything—I was a mother. An instant mother, with a seven-year-old daughter. (And do you know, that to this day, no one has ever looked at the two of us and suggested we might be sisters?)

An instant mother! Suddenly, all my games, all my dreams, and all my childhood were coming true. Without any more preparation than I had when I strapped that poor cat into the baby buggy, I was now in the same predicament. Only it was worse. I had a kid, not a cat. And my mother was nowhere to be found.

I was on my own, a grown-up woman (or so it appeared to the rest of the world) with a real-live child who happened to have all the needs of a real-live child and a penchant for calling the woman married to daddy "mommy."

It was a little more than I had bargained for.

My father had trained me to believe that I could do anything I wanted to if I tried hard enough, so that any failures in life (God knows I could never wear contact lenses) were due to a personal lack of perseverance. With this in mind did I become a stepmother. Holly Golightly meets Auntie Mame.

I was, of course, determined to become the world's best stepmother, despite the fact that my mother had not given me any training in this area. It took a lack of foresight on her part, true, but it was beyond her imagination that I would become an instant mother. She brought me up to marry a medical student. Or, if worse came to worse, a law student. So when it did happen to me, I was without legal or medical aid, let alone parental guidance. Mother always told me I would meet and marry Prince Charming. She neglected to tell me he would have a child from a previous marriage.

While I was reasonably sure my new daughter was wash and wear, I was not aware of much else. I didn't even know to punch our birthdates into my little Kosmos computer to check the compatibility of our biorhythms. I simply rolled up my silk sleeves (I was so dumb I didn't even know not to wear silk around kids) and dived in—head first. Look out, daddy: I can do this better than anyone in the world.

I was wrong.

Who Are These Children And What Am I Doing Here?

If you marry a person with children, it's only a matter of time. Sooner or later it will come to you. Perhaps in the first early moments, perhaps in the depths of a dark night, perhaps in the middle of a good, hot shower, or a mental walk through your new life. Then it will happen, maybe without warning: the giant question of all eternity. The question you had, until now, forgotten to ask yourself.

Who are these children and what am I doing here?

Granted, those are really two questions. Undoubtedly, they will come to you as one, along with several other questions, including, *What have I done? Is it too late? Am I mad?* and *Where's my mother?* They are not necessarily the first questions that pop into the mind of a stepparent, but they should be.

To most of us, especially when we're in love, there's a quaint romanticism involved in being a stepparent. It reeks of lace collars, antimacassars, and Christian duty—maybe even sainthood. The notion of taking some motherless child into your home and heart is as romantic as you can get. It's a tradition fostered by the movies, the books, and the Victorian notions of our childhoods. True, the homeless waifs in the movies always had big eyes, hearts of love, and nice manners. And they were left parentless due to a hurricane, shipwreck, or plague rather than a divorce. But who are we to question an act of God? We are merely to take the homeless bugger to our hearts, give him a hot meal and a lot of love, and watch him grow into an integral part of our families. There's something about homeless children and kittens that gets us all right in the old mushbox. So it's quite feasible that when you found out your beloved was a parent from a previous marriage, you had romantic rather than realistic feelings. If love is blind, prospective stepparents are blind and deaf.

If you're normal, you may not realize what happened to you until much later. You may not even come to your senses until you've been hit repeatedly with a blunt instrument, or an instant child or two. *After* the wedding and the tossed rice, after the honeymoon and the shared secrets, you may suddenly find yourself asking the most incredible questions. Who are these children anyway? What am I doing here? Funny, but you never thought to ask before.

I, for one, never considered those two questions until the third year of my marriage. I was so busy trying to be the kind of stepmother that I thought I should be, and do the kind of things I thought I should be doing, that I refused to admit to anyone—least of all myself—that I had walked into a terrible mess which left me with burning doubts and answerless questions.

Before my marriage, members of my family were not without their warnings and advice. My Aunt Lynn gave me the best advice of anyone and I ignored her. ("Be nice, Susan, but don't get involved. Take things as they come, but don't try to change anything.") My mother did a lot more cluck-clucking about what a terrible thing it was to marry a man with a child from a previous marriage. (Although we sent scores of copies of our engagement announcement from the *New York Times* to San Antonio for distribution among family and friends, my mother quickly burned all the papers because they mentioned my husband's previous marriage and child. Mother didn't want her friends to know her daughter couldn't find a single man.) My husband's daughter was categorically banned from the ceremony. Romantic-notion-me wanted the seven-year-old child to be part of the wedding, to have a dress matching mine, and to be on hand for all the traditions. It was my mother who had a true sense of realism and knew that Amy might stand by my side, but she wouldn't do it quietly. Only my mother was smart enough to know that a seven-year-old child was a seven-year-old child—not a short adult—and would be too much for any of us to cope with.

I never conceded that Amy took some coping until two years later when I had ulcers and a penchant toward planning her murder. It was only then that I stood back and took a hard look at how my life had changed and was able to wonder who this child was and what I was doing with her.

WHO ARE THESE CHILDREN?

• These children are the product of a former marriage in which your current mate was once an active partner. Unless these children were adopted, they came the usual way. (If they are adopted, you better believe they would have come the usual way if they could have.) It took two to tango. And your spouse tangoed. If you cannot admit this and accept a former sexual intimacy with another partner, you're not doing too well. (Go back to Engaged. Do not collect a Husband.)

• These children are part of your spouse's life. They always will be, even after the child-support payments stop. Now they are also part of your life.

• These children may not mean as much to him (her) as you do, but they do exist. He (she) has responsibilities toward them. By marrying a person with children you marry into those responsibilities. The children will not disappear, nor will the problems of raising them.

• These children are capable of ruining your relationship with your new mate, wrecking your marriage, and causing you severe personal handicap. Stepchildren do not, like cigarettes, come with a warning from the surgeon general. Anyone who underestimates their influence in a second marriage is deceiving himself. Open your eyes to the facts.

WHAT AM I DOING HERE?

• Making a better life than the one I had before I met him (her) despite the hard road ahead.

• Saving the souls of the precious little ones. (Careful, we've seen this movie before. If this is your answer, you're in a lot of trouble.)

• Waiting for the kids to grow up so we can be free. (Good luck. What are you going to do until they grow up?)

Obviously, there aren't too many good answers to the second question. If you didn't marry for better or for worse, you may find you married simply for worse. If you can't live without your spouse, then you know what you're doing here. And much as you'd rather be someplace else some of the time, deep down inside you really do know what you've done and will only regret it some of the time.

It's possible that had I asked myself these important questions before we were married, I might have changed my mind. I doubt it. Emotional nearsightedness may well be a protective device that shields us from the painful truth, allowing us to tackle mountains we didn't know were treacherous. Had anyone told me how difficult being a stepparent was going to be, I wouldn't have believed him. I was unwilling to see anything but what I chose to see, so that by the time I did realize what had happened to me, I was too much in love with my husband to walk out (although I have since been tempted).

Only after I accepted that I was here to stay did the dangerous questions take a new twist in my mind. *What Am I Doing Here?* turned into *How Could You Do This To Me?* Clearly, it was my husband's fault that I was a stepmother, so it was totally his fault that I was in this predicament. She's his kid, right? So when anger or confusion or simple hurt feelings get the best of me, I am quick to lay blame on my husband. Me victim; he culprit. Which isn't very adult at all—but that never stopped me.

The natural parent has no idea that the stepparent is constantly reexamining and doubting. If he has never been a stepparent, he usually doesn't understand that you never guessed the ramifications of marrying a person with children. "She *knew* you had a daughter" is my husband's first wife's favorite answer to any of my problems. Yes, I knew he had a daughter. But I never knew what having a daughter meant. And until the stepparent is able to find a place for herself in the New American Family, and accept the role of a stepparent, she will never find answers to the questions that haunt.

The New American Family

Mother was pretty quick to tell us that nice people didn't get divorced. That was twenty-five years ago, when we all grew up in families with mothers and fathers, brothers and sisters, even a dog, cat, and hamster. (My family also had a rapid succession of white mice and guinea pigs.) Sure, there were one or two kids at school who had divorced parents, maybe even had stepparents—but it was pretty much a topic to be whispered about. Nice people didn't get divorced.

Today they do. And with them the family structure of the country has changed so drastically that those who recognize a family with a mother, father. brothers, sisters, and pets may be witnessing a rare oddity worth study. The family as we remember it from our childhood has just about disappeared. Divorce, remarriage, and recoupling are part of the American way of life. According to a study by *Newsweek*, one out of every three, in some states two, marriages ends in divorce. Seventy-five percent of the formerly married will remarry. More than half of them have children from their first marriage. Not all children grow up in a family with their natural parents still married to each other. Few children have only two sets of grandparents.

The New American Family is the combined family, a montage of bits and pieces from other families now joined together in holy pandemonium. There are parents, stepparents, ex-wives, ex-husbands, children and stepchildren, grandparents and extra grandparents plus a variety of aunts and uncles and cousins that create a new, larger, more loosely constructed version of the old-fashioned extended family. Who's related to whom and how—and for how long—can be a matter too confusing to unravel.

When we marry a man or woman with children from a previous marriage, we not only marry that child, but an ex-spouse, another set of grandparents, and a variety of aunts, uncles, and interpersonal relationships. And when the ex-spouse remarries a person with children from a previous marriage, they too become part of the family. And the sisters and the brothers and the parents of the newlyweds are also absorbed into the web of interconnecting lives which now make up the New American Family. It's like a Gilbert and Sullivan operetta. One could almost draw overlapping circles through the living rooms of America to connect daddy B with children B who live with mommy A who remarried daddy C who sees his own children only on weekends but they too are a part of the family D and C. Thus, in a roundabout way, we all become related. If my husband's daughter has a stepsister through her mother's remarriage, am I not related to that stepsister by the very fact that she is part of Amy's life and part of the decision-making process that interconnects our families?

What we have created is a lot of new relationships for a lot of strangers who, finding themselves related, think they are supposed to act and feel like family . . . much to their consternation.

The Stepmother: Married to the man who has children from a previous marriage, she has one of the hardest roles in the current structure of the American family, simply because she has almost no role. Despite the divorce and remarriage rate, society has yet to make room for extra mommies, so the traditional one-per-customer attitude usually leaves the stepmother feeling hurt and angry. The custodial stepmother, who lives full time with the children of her husband, does have a place in the lives of her stepchildren and does not suffer the problems of being left out of a previously formed and closed society. The custodial stepmother usually suffers more of the problems common to adoptive parents than to noncustodial stepmothers.

The Stepfather: The man who marries a woman with children of her own moves into a home prepopulated—but already structured—in the traditional American manner: one mommy and one daddy. While there are in fact two daddies, their roles are reversed because the natural father is not the custodial parent.

Significant Other: There are a tremendous number of liaisons in which men and women take the role of a stepparent without the benefit of marriage and title. When parents live together, their children form step-relationships with the new partners on a more shallow level than with a remarried parent because the children are able to continue their fantasy that after this liaison, the natural parents will seek each other out and remarry. Significant Others may therefore be accepted into step-relationships until they become stepparents. (See Engaged Versus Married, page 102.)

Step-Grandparents: The parent of a stepparent is a stepgrandparent and the transition period from grandparent (or plain old parent) to step-grandparent may be so instant that their newfound status in the family can be a considerable shock. Step-grandparents are mostly plagued with feelings of confusion, knowing they have little interest in the children of another marriage yet not wanting to be unfair by favoring their natural grandchildren. They then suffer the double bind of loyalty to a former spouse and difficulty accepting a divorce, and perhaps a remarriage. Mother-in-law jokes will soon be replaced by step-grandparent jokes and laugh lines devoted to the family with two or three mothers-in-law.

Stepaunts and Uncles: By the time you get to aunts and uncles, the confusion evens out a little bit. Although many brothers and sisters, especially in close families and families living in the same city, will have definite feelings about both sets of spouses, these feelings are not usually carried over to the children. Aunts and uncles can find themselves in the same position as step-grandparents, but are usually more flexible.

Part-Time Parents: The part-time parent most common in the New American Family is the noncustodial parent who sees his own children only when legislated by law or allowed by a former mate. The part-time father may well be full-time stepfather, but must also deal with his own children in an entirely different (and part-time) relationship. While there are noncustodial mothers, and the **number** is rising, women who choose to give up the daily care of their children usually do so for good cause and therefore are unlikely to become custodial stepmothers to someone else's children. It is not unheard of for women to take part-time roles in raising their children.

Part-Time Children and Stepchildren: In some cases, natural children are split between two custodial parents and are reunited on a part-time basis. Or, they may be combined with another person's children from a previous marriage to form a blended or reconstituted family—like the Brady Bunch. They may also enter a step-relationship in which the natural parent and stepparent subsequently have their own children, making a stepsibling combination.

The Story of Cinderella

Amy and her friend Desiree were playing in the front yard as I drove up.

"Who is that?" asked Desiree as I walked into the house.

"That's my stepmother," replied Amy.

"Oouououou, you have a stepmother?" asked the child with the unfortunate name.

"Oh, it's okay, she's not wicked or anything."

Desiree, who did not look the least bit like Audrey Hepburn and who was sinking quickly to her Waterloo in my estimation, accepted Amy's word on the subject and allowed herself to be introduced, although she would not shake hands. Desiree obviously knew the unwritten law of remarriage: stepmothers have cooties.

Amy and I had previously made a deal wherein she would be called my "sometimes daughter" and I would be called her "other mother" in an attempt to get away from the words stepmother and stepdaughter. Amy swears she's stuck to her side of the bargain and only uses the word step to refer to stairs, but the day after meeting Desiree, I was introduced to Amy's piano teacher.

"Rosemary, this is Suzy, my stepmother."

I winced, resigned to my fate. I had already introduced myself at Amy's school as her "other mother," much to everyone's confusion and consternation. The world, I soon learned, is not ready for other mothers. The world, having endured centuries of Cinderella, is only prepared to accept what it knows.

"Stepmother" needs no further explanation. Not only does it quickly sum up divorce by stating that a child's parents have remarried, but it passes judgment on our worst fears. A stepmother is what Cinderella had. All stepmothers eat their husbands' young, cackle at dawn, and thrive on the blood of innocent youngsters who forgot to say their evening prayers. Even if a stepmother appears to be okay, one can't be too careful . . . it's always good to ask if she's tame.

You can blame all this on Cinderella. That kid with her glass slipper has forever colored our perceptions of the word stepmother. One thousand years of story telling, in every language and culture, has reinforced a meaning that no one can escape. There isn't a person alive who doesn't know about Cinderella and is not influenced by her definition of a stepparent. If you played a word association game with anybody—anybody at all in the whole world—and said the word stepmother, the two automatic responses would be Cinderella and/or wicked.

There appears to be no way to undo the deed. Even a modern fairy tale about a greedy ex-wife could not wipe out the sympathy we have for Cinderella. The things that are ingrained in childhood are the hardest to rethink, and we were all carefully taught our prejudices about step-mothers at a very early age. Perhaps if we each reexamined the story of Cinderella, now that we are stepparents, and passed the story on from another point of view, it would make a difference. After all, no one has ever considered that the stepmother might have been justified in her behavior. Maybe Cinderella deserved everything she got!

The Revised Tale of Cinderella

... Papa returned Saturday afternoon with his new wife and her two daughters, Priscilla and Augustina. He was anxious to get back, for he had been gone a long, long time. And he missed his daughter, Cinderella.

"Ah, Ella" he thought fondly, "are you going to be a happy little girl! I have brought you a new family that will make us happy again."

She hasn't been happy in a long, long time, he mused, saddened with the thought of his wife Marie who had died of the plague four years earlier. Since then, he and Cinderella had tried to make their own happiness. But it had been difficult.

He was still lost in thought about the sadness of be-ing without a wife when the coach drew up to the castle. The coachman hurried to help the new family across the

*drawbridge and into their new home where Cinderella and
the staff were waiting.*

*"Ella," Papa chimed as he took her in his arms, "we
are all going to be very, very happy again. Now we can be
a family. I have brought home my new wife, Clarinda, and
her daughters. Now you will have playmates and school-
mates. And someone to make the meals and tuck you in
bed at night."*

*Immediately, Clarinda (papa's new wife), threw off
her muff and rushed forward, thrusting her hand out to
Ella, touching her gently.*

*"How do you do, Ella? I'm so glad to meet you at
last. I've heard so much about you. I know this is difficult
for you, my dear. It's going t͠ be hard for all of us, at first. I
am not your mother and will never be able to replace her. I
know she was a wonderful woman. But I am here to be
your friend. My daughters are here to be your friends. I
hope that in time you will grow to love us and accept us
into your family. My, what nice eyes you have. Just like
your beautiful mother's."*

Are you running with me? I mean, this lady is your
basic loving and understanding trying-to-do-the-best-she-
can-stepmother. She could be you or me. The fact is, the
fairy tale leaves out all the good information about Cinderella's stepmother and dotes on how wicked, selfish and
cruel she is. Boo!

In most versions of this tale, the stepmother doesn't
even have a name.

It's completely possible that it all happened just like
I told it and that Cinderella was a complete bitch—leaving
her stepmother a bitter and angry woman who was able to
extend herself no further. After several years with a difficult child, any stepmother may get testy—even if she was

the original fairy godmother. In short, we don't know the other side of the story. It's just possible that we all would have done the same things Cinderella's mother did and been justified in doing them. (They just didn't have boarding school in those days.)

Yet, because the world is loath to take into account the problems of stepparenting, we have spent centuries hating a woman we know little about and hating ourselves as stepparents because of our childhood perceptions. Have you ever thought what Cinderella's stepmother could tell us now? Perhaps if she had kept a diary, or published hers, we would all be in a better situation today. Imagine this.

Saturday—Well, another weekend is here, hopefully to be better than the last. Cinderella was so uncooperative last weekend, just sat around sulking all day. She spends more and more time in that damn damp cellar and I'm terrified she'll catch her death of a cold. This weekend I've filled the days with plenty to do so she can join in the fun. I hope things work out better. We're all getting a little strained bending over backwards for someone who doesn't even try to meet us half way.

Sunday—What a weekend! The dressmaker came to fit the girls with new gowns, but Cinderella went into a big snit saying we were insulting her by calling for the dressmaker. She says she can make clothes for everyone in the family better than the dressmaker and that it's her only creative outlet. She actually accused us of taking her only pleasure away from her! I don't really know how to handle the situation because last time we had an outburst like this she bitched and bitched about how much work it was to redecorate my room even though she volunteered to do it as a birthday gift: she kept saying she was a slave and was trapped in this insufferable job, refused to come out of the room until the work was done, and wouldn't eat a thing. It was dreadful. This girl just doesn't seem to know what she wants. What a problem...

Alas, we never knew the other side of the story and we are stuck with Cinderella as she was handed down to us, glass slipper, fairy godmother, and all. It's unlikely that Cinderella's stepmother will ever get an even break. It is possible, however, that future generations of children will be told the tale with a disclaimer (the names have been changed to protect the innocent dum-de-dum-dum) stating that all stepmothers are not like the one portrayed in the book. Short of that disclaimer, each stepparent—particularly each stepmother—must enter the arena of parenting with the knowledge that the harmless little story of her youth is now affecting her relationship with her stepchildren and also influencing her own image of a stepmother.

The wicked stepmother role is laid before us and we find it easy to slip into. The opposite of perfection seems immediately to be wicked. When I must reprimand my stepdaughter I automatically slip into the path Cinderella neatly set up for me: "Your wicked stepmother wishes to announce that you have one half-hour in which to clean up your room or suffer the consequences." Cinderella has programmed me to undermine my own efforts. Cinderella has taught my subconscious that all stepmothers are wicked. Cinderella has made all our lives miserable.

2.
Congratulations!
You're a Parent

Defining Yourself
As A Stepparent

As a newly initiated or about-to-be stepparent, you owe yourself and your new family a definition of your role. More than likely the definition will change with time as you come to deal with the nuances of your own personal situation. While combating the myth of Cinderella deep inside yourself, and the children, you are screaming for your own identity and possibly unsure of how to assume it. Most first-time stepparents are so wrapped up in wanting to be perfect that they fail to see the need for instant identity.

You need to know who you are and what you want to be to these children when you enter the relationship;

they need to know what to expect. The children are looking to you for the rules. If you don't lay them out immediately, they may well assume there are no rules and go about testing you to find the limits. Children constantly test all adults as it is, so there's no need making that procedure more elaborate. As a stepparent, you might as well walk in with your self-esteem high, the rules of the game in your hand, and the knowledge that things will always change.

Before you even meet the children, try to get an idea of what your role will be so that you can begin to form your definitions of the role you will be taking. Ask yourself these questions:

- Will the children be living with me permanently?
- If not, how often will I see them?
- How old are the children?
- What is the condition of their natural parent?
- What am I prepared to give to these children?
- What do they need?
- Am I to be a substitute father (mother) or a friend?
- Are religious differences going to affect this relationship?
- Do I feel too old for this responsibility?
- Is money related to my feelings about the children, their natural parent, and my new spouse?
- How will they get along with my own children?
- Are these the kind of children I am proud to be related to or do they embarrass me?
- Will my family be able to accept these children?
- Am I finished with my relationship with my former spouse?
- How do I feel about his (her) former spouse?
- Will my life change significantly because of these children? Do I resent that?

Once you have established in your own mind who and what you are going to try to be to the kids, you must convey this definition to them. Children need, and want, to know the rules. They will then decide if they can live with them or not. But they need some perimeters to begin with.

Enter your step-relationships with the rules clearly defined in your mind. Discuss them with your spouse so you're sure of his (her) support. The kids need to know their parents present a united front on the major issues. Lay out the rules and stick to them. The more consistency, the better. Make the rules simple and clean-cut, with the punishment appropriate but obvious. The do's and don'ts of the relationship have to be established and enforced if you don't expect to get walked—or stomped—on from the beginning. Once you've lost the first few battles, it's more difficult to get back the ground you've conceded.

As instant parents, we all want to be perfect. We want our new children to like—and, we hope, love—us. We want everyone to live happily-ever-after-just-like-in-the-movies. So when the child punches you in the stomach, you are confused. Do you (a) punch him back, or, (b) laugh it off, saying, "kids will be kids?" Don't answer too quickly—your future is at stake.

Those of us from the strong definition school of behavior have only one answer: hit back. Our rule book says not to hit the stepparent. *You do not hit me and expect to get away with it* is a pretty good rule for any parent. Enforce the rule immediately, and you probably won't get punched in the stomach again. Let it go, and you could have a severe problem. The rules should cover more than physical violence. A child may never punch you in the stomach. He may not fold his napkin on his lap, say thank you, clean up his room, or keep his elbows off the table. It's up to you to show him what the rules are and how he can live with them, and you.

The Dating Parent
And The Married Parent

Behavior of all parties involved in a step-situation may change from the dating stage to the married stage, although the greatest change can be expected from the children. Children may well accept you into their family circle as daddy's girl friend or mommy's friend (Uncle Dave?), but then it comes time for Uncle Dave to become Daddy Dave, the mood may change. This happens because deep inside the child has never let go of the possibility that his parents will be reunited. He may like you fine, but he knows his parents should be together so their lives can go back to the way they were before the divorce. He may never talk about this secret fantasy of his, but he harbors it just as does every other child of divorce. When one parent remarries, the child suddenly realizes that his little dream is not going to materialize. It's possible that he is confronting the reality of the divorce for the very first time—even if the divorce took place many years earlier.

As Amy was concluding her first summer visit with us, she took it upon herself to have a heart-to-heart, wo-man-to-woman talk with me one morning while I braided her hair. "Do you like my mommy?" she began hesitantly. Now what kind of a dummy could she think I was? I mean, really.

"Of course I like your mommy," I reassured her. I didn't have much reason to dislike her mommy at that time, so it wasn't even a lie. (I'd have lied if I had to.)

Satisfied with my answer she announced, "Good. Then you and daddy can move to California and live with us and we'll all be together. Daddy can marry mommy again and you can take care of me." (Stepmother as baby-sitter. Why didn't I see the handwriting?)

Appalled, and too new at being a stepmother to want to tackle this myself, I quickly called my husband to explain the facts of life to his seven-year-old. It all ended in sobs of tears and her confession that she didn't understand why Mike would refuse to marry his former wife if he still liked her and why I would object when I too liked her.

The First Meeting

I approached my first meeting with Mike's daughter the way someone twenty years younger might approach Christmas. I couldn't wait. It was an exciting, joyous time in my life. Every day I prepared a little more for her coming: I cleaned out a shelf in the medicine cabinet for her things; I made her an overnight bag for our weekend trips. I spent lunch hours in the library reading the newest children's books and checking out the good ones for her bedtime stories. I began to create the Amy Sheets—red flowered sheets which I handstitched with a bouquet of calico flowers and her name.

Mike spoke very little about her likes and dislikes, so she never had a personality of her own to me. I was free to make her what I wanted her to be—which is what I did. I interpreted my own childhood in terms of someone seven years old and set to work making the world perfect. I bought and did for her what I myself would want. And I was having a wonderful time. Youth may indeed be wasted on the young, but childhood has been created by adults with the money to buy what they always wanted. Life could not have been better.

Three days before she arrived I began to panic. The sheets weren't finished and I was beginning to resent the hours spent over the sewing machine. What if she were difficult? Demanding? What if she didn't like me? (I never considered that I might not like her.) What if she were just like her mother? What if, what if? All the questions I had never thought about before came to me. I had been in a fantasy world and I didn't even know it. The first meeting began to feel like a date with the devil. I picked fights with Mike. I wasn't sure I wanted to get married. My stomach hurt. I wanted my mommy.

It was arranged that Mike would go to the airport to get Amy, giving him a little bit of privacy and a chance to answer her questions about me. After all, we were presenting her with a fait accompli. I stayed home with my stomachache and a terrible case of I-have-nothing-to-wear.

What to wear on the occasion of meeting your stepchildren is not something mother ever discussed when she spoke about white shoes after Memorial Day and always being safe in a little black dress. Should I wear jeans and a T-shirt so I would look like the real me? Should I try one of my hostess gowns—perhaps the turquoise silk? Maybe the ivory lounging pajamas—for the glamorous mother look.

Makeup? I wouldn't normally wear any on a Sunday evening. How much makeup? False eyelashes maybe? My contact lenses? Maybe just some tinted glasses. Do I risk getting mascara in my contacts? Was my manicure perfect? Did I perhaps need a pedicure?

The questions never ended. I finally settled for a pair of blue jeans, a T-shirt, and the contact lenses. (I have never worn the T-shirt or the contacts since that day.)

Mike and Amy arrived. I immediately abandoned the welcome hug idea. She stood in the middle of the living room, hugging her purse to her chest in clutched fists. Her hair was stringy and dirty. Her T-shirt (a gift from me) was too small, and didn't match her skirt. I hated her immediately. She didn't look anything like her pictures. She was not a miniature me. One look at her and my body went tense. I awkwardly stuck out my hand for a proper shake.

"This kid has terrific mousy brown hair," was all I could think. I couldn't wait until she was old enough for me to start frosting it.

"Gee, you're tall," she whispered.

I'd heard that one before so I barely blanched. Maybe she thought I was a giant and would gobble her up. (In retrospect, that would have been a very smart thing to do.) But I had already decided on being the perfect step-mother, so we took her out to dinner instead.

I'm not really sure how I got through the first few minutes. I did unpack her things and we did end up in a restaurant having a good time. I did refuse to let her sleep with her daddy and I did live through it all. Somehow.

After dinner we returned to the apartment and opened the sofa bed to unfurl the Amy Sheets. I awaited her delight. "Ouuuuu," would have been sufficient.

Total silence. Nothing. At last she spoke, "Daddy, will you read me a story?"

I kissed her good night and retreated to our bedroom. I considered crying but thought I shouldn't act like a child when we had just gained another child. I decided to be a good sport. This was the beginning of my tucking away my emotions so they would settle into hurt and anger. I didn't know until years later that had things been done differently on the first meeting, we all would have been happier.

Plan the First Meeting Carefully. You must decide ahead of time what kind of meeting this will be and what it is to accomplish, then plan the meeting to suit your needs. If you are already married and are presenting children you've never met with a fait accompli, you must arrange the first meeting differently than if you are merely a serious love interest or significant other with only the possibility of becoming a stepparent. Your role in relation to the children should be defined from the first meeting.

Choose Your Territory Carefully. Neutral ground is the best place for a first meeting: a restaurant, park, or place of entertainment. Your home is a strange place to children who do not know you, and you are the stranger. Minus ten points. His home is considered their territory—they may well immediately think of you as the intruder. Not perfect. McDonald's? Great. The movies and dinner? Perfect. Go public and there won't be any scenes. Go public and there are no former memories shadowing the event. Besides, if you meet in a restaurant, you won't have to worry about what to say. Everyone knows it's rude to talk with your mouth full of food.

Do Something. The best first meeting is one in which everyone can do something that will precipitate a good time and ease the conversation along. The first meeting with the children should not be like sorority rush, or a job interview. You do not have to stand before a board of children and list your qualifications for being their stepparent. The minute everyone does something together and has a good time, a bond is formed. And bonds build relationships. The first meeting should entail any activity that generates its own conversation and allows each family member to take his mind off the strangeness of the other.

Plan Options. Flexibility. You may plan your first meeting perfectly only to find your plans do not suit the occasion. Have a backup plan or two. Consider all sides of the issue, all ways of tackling the meeting. Don't settle for your first workable plan and don't let your feelings be hurt if things don't follow your master plan.

Meet the Children With Their Natural Parent. For the first meeting, there should be no reason for you to have to have to greet the kids alone. After things get going, you may want to talk to them alone—but you shouldn't have to meet them without the support of their natural parent. Make sure you and the real parent agree on the role you are taking in the children's lives so you can both establish the step-identity from the first meeting. Make sure you are backed one hundred percent by your mate; your strength will be terribly undermined if the children do not see their natural parent supporting you from the beginning, even if you are just a date for the day. No support? Consider a new mate, or an annulment before it's too late.

Rehearse Your Greetings. Plan how you want to meet the children and what you will first say to them. If you're scared or nervous try not to show it . . . after all, the kids are also scared and nervous and it's your job as the adult to put them at their ease. You may very well be able to do that by admitting you were scared to meet them—but don't be too honest. All you have to do is win them over. If you hate kids and want no part of these, you don't have to say so. They'll catch on quickly enough from your manner and will react to your feelings. If you are enthusiastic about meeting them, show it without going overboard. Also remember that at the time of the first meeting, they have more reason to dislike you than you do them. You are confident that you can win them over. They think you are a monster. Try to greet them in a way that overshadows any preconceived hates. Shake hands with any child over ten. Consider shaking hands with any child over seven. Touch them as soon as possible if you want to warm things up. Failure to touch them signifies fear.

Don't Worry If It Didn't Go Well. What? You mean you really expected it to go well? Now really. Sure, we all have our hopes, but we've all got to be prepared for the social barriers of the situation. It's very possible that the first meeting will not go as well as you've planned it. Be prepared for that, but don't let it get in your way. Chances are the first meeting will go less well than you planned it but better than you thought it did. If the first meeting is a disaster, think nothing of it. This is an emotional situation and time is on your side. On the other hand, if subsequent meetings are so disastrous that you wonder how much more you can take, it could be time to reassess the relationship.

Wearing the right thing for your first meeting is important because you need to feel comfortable. You will have plenty of other things on your mind at the first meeting; your clothes should not be one of them. Children associate fashion with power. If you're wearing jeans and a fishing shirt, you could be a peer. If you're wearing a suit you are definitely a grown-up. That's not to say you should wear a suit to McDonald's for your first meeting, it's just that most people don't know that children respond to clothing and associate it with power. On my first meeting with my husband's daughter, I chose what I normally would have worn on any typical Sunday evening: a pair of jeans and a T-shirt. I thought it would be phony or pretentious to get dressed up. I was wrong. Many days after Amy's arrival, when I was dressing for an occasion I thought warranted curled hair, makeup, and panty hose, Amy took a good hard stare at me and announced; "You know, you're kinda pretty after all. I like you better like this." Children are suckers for glamour, and don't you forget it. (Teenagers, however, are quick to criticize.) When dressing for your first and subsequent meetings, pick clothes suited to the ages of the children. I ended up with a complete mommy wardrobe that I wore only when Amy was in town. Everything was wash and wear, inexpensive, and completely dispensable. I was able to duplicate my own "look" without having to worry about dry cleaning bills. If you can't play with the kids because you'll run your stockings, rumple your pants' crease, or mess up your hair, you're never going to make it as even a part-time parent.

I hope you'll be too busy having a good time on your

first meeting to worry about what you're going to say to these children, but it doesn't hurt to be prepared. Make a list of topics that you're good at which might interest children of their age so you can quickly fill in those terrible empty spaces that sometimes happen in new conversations. You do not have to chatter incessantly, but it won't hurt to have some topics tucked into your mind. (See *How To Talk To A Child,* page 162.) The children will probably have a lot of questions about you and the role you are planning to take in their lives. You may want to answer those questions before the kids ask. If you are not already married, the first thing the kids want to know is how serious your relationship with their parent is. Are you just friends? Is it permanent? Will you be seeing them again? Regularly? Should they invest any of themselves in getting to know/like/love you? Will you be leaving and possibly hurting their feelings? While you don't have to have a checklist of these questions in your hand, the first meeting is a time to tell the children exactly where you fit into their lives. It's also a good time to tell them what role you will be playing. "I can never replace your father (mother)," is exactly what they want to hear. If you do plan to replace the parent, you don't have to say a word.

When it's time to leave the kids after the first meeting, you may experience a bit of awkwardness. Should you hug them? Is a kiss okay? Is shaking hands too formal? Your good-bye should be casual, friendly, and open to any future meeting—in a noncommittal way. "See you guys later" may mean you'll never see them again or that you plan to be a regular part of their lives. Even if the first meeting was disastrous, try to have a cheery good-bye—filled with promise that the next time will be better. Bad good-byes linger as the final memory.

In Case Of War. There will be some instances when the children not only don't want to meet the potential stepparent, but are determined to cause as much trouble as possible in the hopes of splitting up the match. The more children there are in the family, the more chance of them going to war—especially if they're over the age of ten. Kids against stepparents is a rather prevalent theme for B movies. I seem to remember the hot movie of the summer in my youth, *The Parent Trap*, a Hayley Mills story about twins (Hayley played both parts) who ganged up on their parents to prevent their reunion—or something like that. Then I saw another movie, rather recently on a rainy Sunday afternoon, in which the children of the lovers went so far as to go on a hunger strike, and when that didn't work, they ran away from home. They took out a boat in a storm and the little girl got washed into the rocks and was certainly in no shape to apologize. Needless to say, the Italian count took his son and left the English lady with her two kids. (They gave up each other for the sake of their children.) God, my stomach still hurts when I think of that one.

Anyway, the moral of the stories is that every now and then you'll find a kid or two who really doesn't want to be part of his step-family.

If the children are dangerously antagonistic at the first meeting, you have a few choices:

• Give them a few more chances before you make any decisions.

• Pack your bags and leave immediately, saying you're too young to cope with this bullshit.

• Put your foot down: cause an even bigger scene and make it clear that their behavior will not be tolerated.

• Threaten to send them out of your lives. Don't threaten to leave, because that's exactly what they want you to do. The kids never consider that you will let them go, so you just may have to shock them into being polite or being dumped.

Often the children are just pushing to see how far they can get. The kids who are just pushers and the real troublemakers will be readily distinguishable after the first showdown. If you are determined that the little brats won't win their game, be careful to see what you're fighting for. It's possible you're now into the challenge of the fight and want to win for your pride's sake. A sensible look at the real situation may show you that it's not worth fighting over. If you see the children as miserable, conniving, troublemaking little brats, and she (he) says the kids are angels—or to give them a break for all they've been through—you can plan on plenty of trouble for years to come. Maybe you should reconsider this marriage. If it's too late to reconsider, perhaps you should begin to negotiate a workable peace, while you still have your sanity.

In the stepparent's search for perfection, he (she) often thinks a present is appropriate for the first meeting. Nothing like a little bribery to start the ball rolling. Wrong. Unless it is the child's birthday, or some gift-giving holiday, it's very wrong to bring a gift to the first meeting. If it is a gift-giving occasion, let the natural parent sign the card. The card will be the child's indication of how much you figure into his life. If the gift is from dad and Sue rather than just dad, the kid knows right up front. Sue should never bring a separate present. Bribery does have its place in this world, but it doesn't buy respect from children and more than anything else you need these kids to respect you. Lay off the gifts, especially in the beginning.

What They Should Call You

Never has the name game been more complicated than it is in second families. Obviously, more than getting someone's attention is at stake. Respect, love, and ego are tightly woven into the choice of a name used by a stepchild for a stepparent.

It's common for the children to call the stepparent by his (her) given name. When the kids meet the would-be parent before the wedding, they are usually introduced on a first name basis and the name sticks. With very young children, and children searching for more from their stepparent than a place to sleep, daddy or mommy is added to the given name. (For three years of Amy's life she had a Daddy Ben and a Daddy Mike.)

There are some times when the new parent is outright called mom or dad or an equivalent thereof. This frequently happens in a family where one of the parents died when the child was young, or in cases of abandonment and adoption. Some families use variables of parental titles for all the parents so there may be a mommy and a mom and a dad and a pop, with each adult clearly knowing which is his title.

"If you're going to marry my daddy, then you're going to be my mommy," Amy explained to me shortly after we met. "So I'll just call you mommy." (Maybe learning my name was too hard?)

No one had ever called me mommy, and it was a frightening experience. Did being called mommy change my role? Did Amy need reassurance that she would be mothered? Was I treading on her own mother's territory? Was it right or wrong? Graciously I explained to her that each person in the world had only one mommy and one daddy and that Amy already had two parents. I said I would be her special friend and that she should call me Suzy. Considering she caught me by surprise, I thought I did great.

Amy paid me no heed and called me mommy. After the third day of corrections, I gave up. She seemed to need a mommy and I began to question my original premise. Although I have no stepparents, I do have a friend whom I call Mom. She "adopted" me and took me into her family. I never felt comfortable calling her Mrs. Cohen or Barbara. With my own family two thousand miles away, the Cohen family was there when I needed them. Mom always took care of me when I was sick, advised me when I needed her, and supported me when I needed a family. I never confused her with my real mother; my real mother didn't mind that I called someone she never met Mom. So I began to think about my relationship with Barbara Cohen when Amy started calling me mommy. I just hoped I could do as much for her as Mom had done for me.

It did not work out that gracefully when Amy referred to me as "mommy" to her natural mother—we were all in serious trouble. Amy's mother made it quite clear to her, through her sniffles and tears, that she had only one mother. Amy's reaction was simple: she continued to call me Mommy and was careful to call me Suzy in front of her own mother. I continued to introduce her as "my" or "our" daughter. I never said she was "my husband's daughter," or my "stepdaughter." (Was Cinderella's stepmother ever so thoughtful?)

Children often use intimate mommy and daddy names to manipulate their parents and stepparents. They are well aware of the power of the words and the emotion they bring out in adults. Amy explained to me that it would hurt her stepfather's feelings if she did not call him daddy or Daddy Ben, which she continued to do even after her mother divorced Daddy Ben. But she never called him Daddy Ben around her father. If Amy were angry at her own mother, all she need do was call me Mommy to get a quick and hurt reaction. Amy likewise believed that I shared her stepfather's ego attachment to a title and thought she could hurt my feelings by calling me Suzy.

While I never felt a need to be called mommy, I have had a few bouts of embarrassment after introducing her as my daughter only to have her later call me Suzy. I have since made it clear to her that she can't have it both ways. If she wants to call me by my first name, that's fine—but I refuse to introduce her as my own daughter. She has the choice.

I once interviewed a New York psychiatrist, Dr. Lewis Hott, who told me that the word *step* should be eliminated from our vocabularies and the mother and father titles applied to whichever parent was assuming the role at the time. Parenting is a verb, he announced, and whoever performs the job gets the title. When Amy came to stay with us, I was the mother. When I visited the Cohen family, I was the daughter. It made perfect sense to me. It didn't to Amy's natural mother.

When the conflict arose over what I was to be called, my husband suggested nicknames. I would be "mommynyc" (pronounced *mommynik*—as if I were the latest Soviet spaceship) and Nancee, Mike's first wife, would be "mommyla." He made up the nicknames from the cities we lived in. Although he thought this was the perfect solution, I didn't like it at all. Although many other families do use nicknames, it just didn't gel in our family.

There is a lot to be noted in the loaded meanings of words and how we present ourselves to the outside world. Studies show that when the stepparent and stepchild use family titles and pass themselves off as kin, society and they themselves live much happier-ever-after. You can certainly experiment with this yourself. I know that when I introduce Amy as my daughter and she calls me Mommy, we are treated differently by the real world than when I say she is my husband's daughter and she calls me Suzy. Blood is indeed thicker than water, and society still has little use for step-relationships.

In-law and step-relationships are immediate setups,

like saying you're epileptic. People don't know how to treat you. If you want to return something in a store, tell them that your mother-in-law or stepdaughter gave you the item, and you'll have little trouble exchanging it. Tell them you changed your mind about the color, the style, and the fabric, and they'll say they don't take returns. *Step* is just one of those heavy words that immediately scares people.

Of course, in trying to sidestep the words, we can get in more trouble. You can't try to pass yourself off as something you're not. It's impossible to give a child's medical history if you're not the natural parent—so you shouldn't try. It's also impossible to get society to accept your own new definitions.

For years I tried to be Amy's "other mother," to no avail. I introduced myself at her school as her "other mother." I told her friends I was her "other mother," but the title never stuck. I finally gave up and figured that if I could claim my husband's country home was "ours" that it was only fair to say his daughter was "ours" and be a good sport.

So consider these things when finding the right name:

• *Be flexible.* Remember that this is one area that can change faster than any other in your new relationship. After the kids get to know you better, they may change their name for you. What's agreed on at first may later be discarded as you grow and change together. (One man I interviewed told me that his stepdaughter always called him by his first name until the day he spanked her and immediately called him daddy thereafter.)

• Ask the kids what *they* want to call you. After all, it's their name for you, and they will have so few choices in your relationship that it's nice to leave something to them.

• Don't be influenced by outside pressure. Who cares what your friends and family have to say about what you should be called? This is strictly a family matter. Involve the other members of your family only when it's their turn to get new names. (My mother flinched at becoming an instant grandmother but accepted the honorary title of Grandma Glo.)

• Don't let your ego get in the way. C'mon now, be honest with yourself, do you really want to be called Mommy or does it just flatter your ego? Think about it seriously.

• Speak up immediately if you object to a particular nickname. Don't accept a nickname you hate. You too must live with the name.

Variables That Will Influence Your Role As A Stepparent

There are a few variables that will actually give you a clue as to how much success you will have as a stepparent, or at least serve to point the finger at your more vulnerable spots. Just because there are tested answers to each variable doesn't mean that you will fail as a stepparent or can quit earlier. Sociologic variables are only slightly more scientific than horoscopes: you can only take from them what works for you.

• *Age of the stepparent.* Women under forty are found to cope with stepparenthood better than women over forty. There have been no significant findings in the ages of male stepparents.

• *Age of the children:* Young children accept stepparents more readily than older children.

• *Location of the children:* Children living with the

steprelative adapt better than those living in another family.

• *Religious difference:* Not significant.

• *Financial situation:* Poorer families adapted better to steprelatives than better off families, the theory being that lower income families are used to helping out other relatives and that children are encouraged to have positive attitudes about new faces at the table, in the bathroom, and on the sofa bed. Families in which alimony and child support were no problem and where money was readily available and abundant were not affected by the financial burdens and resentments of second families, so never considered money to be a variable. But money to pay for help can greatly vary your ability to cope.

• *Relationship with ex-spouse:* Important for the former mates and the stepparent.

• *Emotional support of family, society, and significant other:* No man is an island.

The Joy of Step

I used to be one of those people who thought children were cute when they belonged to someone else. Once I attained adulthood, I never wanted a few of my own. I didn't dislike kids, I just thought that I would not be a good mother. I was too impatient, and I liked to spend too much money on clothes. I wasn't crazy about well-balanced meals and I swore off laundry as soon as I could afford to do so.

So it was an unusual shock to find myself in love with Amy and happily adjusting my life to fit my idea of what a good mother should be. I abandoned the Chinese restaurant as the only form of dinner to set on our dinner table and began seriously squeezing vegetables at the green grocer to make sure they were fresh enough for my child to eat. I really got into the whole thing.

I discovered that I was a very good mother. While not as patient as my husband, I am far more patient than I thought I would be. And I remembered enough of the horrors of my own childhood not to inflict them on my new-found child. The mother part of stepmothering agreed with me, and I found several benefits to stepparenting. While they don't overshadow the hardships, they are equal considerations and can't be ignored.

• Stepparenthood gives you a child without a pregnancy.

• Stepparents rarely have to change diapers, or stay up all night with a sick child.

• Stepparents can have the best of two worlds: children some of the time. All other parents are stuck with their children all of the time.

• You may get a child of a different sex. If I never have a daughter of my own, at least I will have had the pleasure of helping to raise someone else's.

• A chance to appraise your own abilities at child raising. Being a stepparent is a lot like renting. You can try it out and see how you like it.

• Being with children teaches you a lot about people who have children. When you've stood in someone else's place, you can better understand his problems.

• Free admission to the children's zoo.

• Plenty of good reason to be silly, just when you thought you were too sophisticated for that kind of thing.

• Dr. Seuss.

The Differences Between Stepmothers and Stepfathers

Two adults at a cocktail party console each other. She complains about the difficulty of being a stepmother. "Yeah," he says, "I know what you mean. I'm a stepfather."

Both nod their heads and consider their new bond. No one else knows what they know. Yet neither understands the problems of the other. Being a stepfather is distinctly different from being a stepmother and the roles are in no way equal because the roles of fathers and mothers are not equal. Despite women's liberation and personal strides in individual households, most mothers still have much more active roles in the lives of American children. And most fathers can still get by with paying the bills and sitting at the head of the table. My father spent our childhood muttering "the father is always the last to know" and "just ask dad when it's time for a buck." His role was disciplinary, economic, and titular. Father may have been the head of the household, but his job was to go to work in the morning and provide for us. Mother did the actual mother work of running a family. I remember being shocked to find out that my father knew how to sew. Daddy certainly never knew when the school bus arrived, or that I hated tomato juice and that Jacquie Jones was my best friend—this week. I considered him useless in household matters.

In the same tradition, a man can marry a woman with children and take a head-of-the-household position without ever becoming involved in the fabric of the children's lives. They look to their natural father for discipline and economic support. He is merely mother's husband and may be able to live in the same house as her children and ignore their existence. While the stepmother may wish she could ignore her husband's children, her chances are not as good. Even on a limited visitation basis, stepmother is written in the book of life for mother work.

Studies show that stepfathers get along better with stepchildren than stepmothers and, conversely, stepchildren prefer stepfathers. There has to be a very important lesson for stepmothers in that fact. The noninvolvement of a father is preferred to a substitute mother worker. (Surely it makes the *Odd Couple* look like the perfect solution. If Felix and Oscar married, their children would accept the new arrangement a lot better than if they chose female mates.) Yet stepmothers are consistently confronted with sexist barriers.

It's as simple as the fact that men marrying women with children do become everyday daddies. They have a place in their stepchildren's lives; their role is somewhat defined for them. While they may not feel that they are head of the household and may have nonparticipatory roles in the growth of their stepchildren, they not only have a place to call home, but the opportunity to carve the relationship of their choosing. No such luck for stepmom. She lives with daddy and the kids have to go to a strange house to be hosted by a strange woman whom they consider an intruder in their family. Suddenly they are forced to compete for daddy's attention; suddenly they know their natural parents will never remarry. Even if stepmom were Auntie Mame, she still isn't part of the family, and her importance to Dad is a constant irritant—especially to older children. By the very fact of location, one steprelative has a better chance than the other.

The difference in step-relationships is not what it appears to be on the surface. Most people think that because stepmothers see their stepchildren less often, and are usually less involved with their daily lives, that they have an easier role than a man who moves into a new home which must house someone else's children whom he lives with daily. Surely the shock is greater for instant stepfathers than for men who have their own children or have been previously married to women with children—but the real difficulties are suffered by the stepmother who does not live with her husband's children.

What Is A Stepparent In The Children's Eyes?

How the children feel about the stepparent is dependent on their age, the availability of both natural parents, the outside influences (such as pressure from grandparents or natural parent), and their relationship with the parent since the death or divorce.

All children consider stepparents to be intruders in some way. The stepparent has come between them and their natural parent and they have been betrayed: the natural parent likes him (her) better! Although I did find three cases of adults who married because their children matched them up and encouraged the marriage, a child can't help but feel some resentment at the change in his life ... even if he was the matchmaker.

After the resentment comes confusion. Does mommy (daddy) still love me? Do they still want me? Do I have a place in this family? Will they ignore me? Do I get in their way? Will I ever have mommy (daddy) to myself again? Will things ever be like they were before? All these are normal questions for a child to continually ask himself ... and maybe his parents, if they are lucky. More commonly, children are quiet about their feelings of resentment and confusion—feeling they are bad if they have such feelings and will be punished for admitting to them—and show their feelings only through misbehavior or manipulation.

One of the most common problems is the child who actually likes/loves his (her) stepparent and feels so guilty about it that he is unable to handle his guilt and confusion. The only thing he (she) knows to do is manipulate a parent (usually the stepparent) into a position of wicked behavior so that he can breathe a sigh of relief and admit that the stepparent is everything Cinderella said she (he) should be. The Cinderella myth hangs heavy with our children and they are much more able to accept wicked/evil stepparents, especially stepmothers, than they are to think that the good fairy was, herself, a stepmother.

In some cases, the child does view the stepparent as the hero or heroine who saves the day. This is usually in families touched by death or abandonment and really hard times. A child who lost a father in infancy may be desperate for a new father and enthusiastically welcome any stepparent into the home...only later to go through the prevalent stepchild syndrome: resentment, confusion, anger, acceptance, liking.

Indeed, all stepchildren go through these stages, in their own time and their own way. Some reach adulthood without having passed out of their anger. There can be no love without liking, and there is seldom any liking without the natural evolution of feelings of resentment, confusion, and anger.

The stepparent is never seen as friend to the stepchild until the child approaches the acceptance stage. Before that the stepparent is intruder, enemy, usurper, and thief. And maybe worse.

The Widowed Versus The Divorced

Kids may be kids, but how they come to be yours (especially when you've never had children of your own) can make an incredible difference in their attitude toward you and subsequently how you get along with them.

A woman marrying a widowed man with children is in a very different situation than the same woman who marries a man with two children from a previous marriage who has custody every other weekend. The fact that a woman never had children of her own and is completely unprepared for parenting is a small point when compared to the feelings of children in regard to gaining a new parent. While the child of divorce now gets an *additional* parent—someone without any particular place in his life and no defined role—the child of death gets a *replacement* parent who is on the job full-time, with a well-defined role and position in the family.

There are many children who simply don't want another parent—be it replacement or additional. Most commonly these are the children with deceased parents who have given more thought to remarriage and have decided that no one could ever replace the deceased parent and that they don't need anyone, anyway—so there. This also happens in families of divorce when a child begins to take on aspects of the role vacated (little girls wife and mother their fathers, little boys become "the man around the house"), but it is not a severe problem because the divorced parent can always be produced. The dead parent, unfortunately, is not available for consultation.

The mere inaccessibility of the dead parent poses the biggest problem to these families. It's not nice to criticize the dead (it's like fooling Mother Nature) so the dearly departed begins to take on characteristics he (she) may have never even had in real life. No one ever denies his (her) glory. The parent loses his (her) human touch and is secure in the world of the gods. A stepparent who must walk the tracks of a ghost is walking on terribly shabby carpet. There is an emotional boundary that is difficult to surpass: perhaps the new spouse must move into a home habitated by the dead spouse—dare he (she) rearrange the furniture, dump that miserable painting of the seagulls on flocked velvet, or repaint the kitchen? The newlyweds may indeed be happy with the changes; the children are hurt and angry. Their ghosts have been insulted. How else can they take such cruelty but to misbehave and reveal their turmoil?

If not careful, second spouses to widows and widowers can quickly take on the *Rebecca* syndrome in which they too will become haunted by the reflection of the dead person in its total unreality. Competing with a living former spouse is difficult enough and not recommended for the mental health; competing with a ghost should be totally out of the question. It's also unfair. I mean, if you have anger to share with the living, it's your duty to spit it out. Not so with the dead.

Stepparents who move into families that idolize their dead have found the only way to deal with the problem is to turn the situation around. "It's true your mother was a wonderful woman and I'm sorry she's not here (boy, am I sorry), but we're going to try this *my* way ... or "Here's another crummy attempt at helping you with your homework ..." until the denigration becomes a joke and the children realize that the new parent is doing just as well as the dead parent.

There is comfort in the fact that in Lucille Duberman's study of reconstituted families (*The Reconstituted Family*), the widowed found greater happiness in second marriages than the divorced. Children of the widowed also proved to be more interested in getting along with the stepparent—many of them needing a replacement parent and not being afraid to admit it or take another into their lives. And again, the fact that the family lives as one unit and functions normally with only one mommy and daddy helps family members, and society, adjust more quickly.

Despite women's liberation, it is a common phenomenon for a widowed man with children to immediately think of remarrying (just what Cinderella's dad did). He may pursue a woman for the wrong reasons: seeing her not so much as bride, but as baby-sitter. Compounding this problem, there are plenty of women who willingly fall into this trap. They need to be needed and are happy to find someone who needs them. Each mate feeds the other's needs without ever forming a personal bond. The marriage will be a difficult one.

The Myth Of
The Perfect Stepparent

Every stepparent enters her role with one thought in mind: she will be the perfect stepparent. It has a lot to do with overcompensation and guilt and, of course, competition. Every second spouse feels the need to prove herself to herself, her spouse, her family, the world in general, but most specifically to the children and the spouse of the former marriage or marriages.

Because second marriages are rooted in first marriages, there is a constant air of stridency ... everyone wants to do better this time. This is endemic to second marriage and will never change. It is compounded, however, by a recent sociological development that will drive all of us —particularly the women—straight into analysis.

What I'm talking about is Super Mom. With the development of Super Mom (sometimes Super Dad), stepparents feel compelled to become extra Super Stepmom (Stepdad)—an almost impossible dream.

The Super Mom (and Dad) myth grew out of the women's liberation movement. While my mother was perfectly willing to accept her life as it revolved around her children and pride herself on being a professional mother, the next generation was being told that they could have it all and do it all. It wasn't enough to take care of the kids, you had to justify your existence by making the best chocolate chip cookies on the block, collecting the most money for the Cancer Society, and making the best costumes for the school play. A Super Mom was never caught without lunch for the kids or clean underwear in the drawers or another Nancy Drew book just when the last one was finished. A Super Dad knew he too could do it all.

The situation reached critical proportions when Super Mom went back to work. She then decided to be Super Mom with super talent, unwilling to give up any of her home duties for fear that she would lose her place in the society of mothers and feel guilty. She didn't believe in the quality time versus quantity time theory—she believed (honestly) that she could do both jobs at once because no one had ever told her that being Super Mom was a full-time professional job.

The pressure is magnified for the new spouse. Not only does she want to be a better wife to her husband than his first wife was (or second or third), but she also wants to be a Super Stepmom. So she is forced to be extra-super. If Super Mom can get up and make breakfast for the kids, then Extra Super Stepmom can get up and make a better breakfast and serve it in a hostess gown with her nails perfectly manicured. In the back of her mind is the fantasy that one child is nudging the other, saying, "Hey, she's even neater than mom. Mom never wears pretty dresses to breakfast." In the back of her mind there is only one goal: beat the myth; do this job better than anyone else. Men often feel the same competition.

It's a bad enough problem to feel you have to compete with your spouse's former mate. It is impossible if you are competing with a myth. The two are not necessarily intertwined: it's one thing if you've built his wife (her husband) into something he (she) is not. That's your problem. It's entirely different if you swallow the media's myth of perfection.

C'mon, you know who she is. You read about her in all the magazines. it's Alice Borden from Boise, Idaho and she helps Ted out during tax season and sells Avon door-to-door when not collecting for the Jerry Lewis Telethon, which is a very worthy cause, but then she also serves as chairman of the local chapter of Women to Save the Seals. She is vice-president of a pest control company she bought with her winnings on "The Price Is Right" and her three healthy (got to be very healthy) children are all studying to be doctors and lawyers. She doesn't have a maid, cooks great beef stroganoff (recipe at the end of the article), and gives Ted an herbal back rub (instructions at the end of the article) on bad days. She has never had a menstrual cramp in her life, doesn't know what a Caesarean section is, and makes dental appointments six months in advance. She plays a mean game of touch football and is still a trim size ten. Do you hate her? God, I hope so!

Yet article after article shows us the emerging woman as a model and sets her up as an example of the right way to be doing things. If she can do it, so can we. She has time for her kids, time for her marriage, time for her career, and somehow time for her sanity. It hardly seems fair to me (maybe because I'm too competitive), but we all sit there looking at the black and white picture of Alice Borden in the kitchen with two of the three kids (the third was out on his paper route and therefore not available) whipping up a casserole and we are pea green with envy. We promise ourselves to be more like Alice Borden. We rededicate ourselves to getting more done. We will get up an hour earlier. We will stay up an hour later. We will make better lists. We will get organized. We too will become super. Maybe even extra-super. We can, we can; we know we can.

If there is a seemingly perfect woman in your family already, the worst thing you can do is try to compete with her. The best thing you can do is develop yourself where your own talents lie and be content in that realm. And if Ms. Perfection is driving you nuts with jealousy and anger, you owe it to yourself (and your husband and the kids) to reexamine her perfection. She probably just appears to be perfect. You probably need to discover that you're fighting a myth. Count it as a myth and live your own life at your own pace. You cannot march to the tune of Alice Borden's drummer. She is a mad, psychotic woman who deserves to have the Teflon burned off her pots and pans. She should be locked away with all people who say they never cry or always answer "fine, thank you" when you ask them how they are, or put in a room with a poster saying Today Is The First Day Of The Rest Of Your Life.

As a stepmother, you cannot try to be the kind of mother you read about in the magazines. (Okay, you can try—but you saw it here first that it's never going to work.) You can't even be the kind of mother you think you ought to be or the kind of mother you always wanted to be, let alone the kind of mother who is better than the kind the ex-wife is or used to be. Unless the natural mother is in some way incapacitated and unable to assume her own mothering duties, you can only be the kind of mother the situation allows. Let your circumstances help you in choosing your definition of a mother. Stop competing with the media's idea of Super Mom. Or, better yet, save it for your own children.

The first step toward a workable relationship with your stepchildren is to ignore everything you've ever read about other mothers, other stepmothers, and other working women and stop fantasizing about what your ideal should be and how to achieve perfection. As hard as motherhood is, stepmotherhood is more difficult. Shadowboxing with myths is counterproductive and dangerous to your mental health. Forget all about Super Mom and Extra Super Stepmom. Relax. Just be yourself. Take it very slowly and the world will be yours.

Stepparent Traps And How to Avoid Them

The myth of Super Mom and Super Stepmom is one of the worst and most dangerous traps stepparents (particularly stepmothers) fall into. In more simple terms it's called fantasizing, and the general fantasy is that you will be a better parent than the natural parent—no matter how good a parent the natural parent is. This fantasy is in the same category as "my marriage would be perfect if my partner were better." Wrong. It's never going to happen. The marriage wouldn't be any better and the problems of being a parent would be no different. You can stop wasting your time on this fantasy and start accepting reality. If you must be perfect, save it for your own children.

Manipulation. A lot of complex and complicated things have been written about child manipulation and the ability of a five-year-old to outsmart an adult. As Machiavellian as it all sounds, children are experts at manipulation. Being a member of a second or stepfamily gives them all the more opportunity to set one adult against another, accomplishing whatever self-satisfying goals they have in mind. Manipulation in step-families is particularly easy (for all members, by the way) because one of the authority figures is missing and because emotions play a greater part in child raising than they did before the divorce.

When the kid says "Mom always let me" when in fact Mom never let him and he knows damn well she would never ever let him, he is playing the fact that the two parents will not confer on the matter until it's too late. When the kid says "Mom never takes us to the movies because she's too busy playing kissing face with Bob," your child is merely manipulating your emotions toward your ex-wife, your anger at her involvement with Bob, and your own need to provide the children with everything their own mother cannot give. Turkey, you have just been taken.

Alas, all is not hopeless. There are some easy ways to know when you're being set up so you can be forewarned and avoid falling into the manipulation trap. If manipulation is a serious problem with any of your children, see a psychiatrist or specialist, or consult a book by one. Otherwise watch out for these telltale signs and get the jump on the pros:

• "My mommy (daddy) said when I come to your house I can ... "

• "My mommy (daddy) knows that I only eat it (do it) when it's done like this ... "

• "My mommy (daddy) always lets me ... "

• "My mommy (daddy) never gives me a chance to ... and I knew you would ... "

• "My mommy (daddy) doesn't do it that way ... "

• "You're my favorite parent because you let me ... "

• (The all-time winner.) "Mommy (daddy) says we can't ... because we don't have the money."

(Warning! The last two are most commonly used only by older children and teenagers.)

No matter how reasonable the request or how terrible the hurt or anger you are suffering, you've got to believe you're being had. You now have a Hobson's choice: be had or take control of the situation by informing the children that you won't fall for their sneaky little tricks and plan to do it your way, whether they like it or not. Answer their manipulative phrases this way:

1. Tough shit.
2. Tough shit.
3. Tough shit.
4. Tough shit.
5. Tough shit.
6. That's really nice, but tough shit.
7. Ha. I'll never fall for that one. Tough shit.

Trying Too Hard. Although Trying Too Hard, which fits into the same category as Going Too Quickly and Expecting Too Much, is a common trap for all stepparents, it particularly afflicts stepmothers and instant mothers, that is, women who have never had children before. Much of trying too hard is related to the fantasy that stepmom can do it better and is more perfect than the natural parent. Trying too hard is the obvious extension of this theory—how else do you prove your stuff but to give those kids the old razzle-dazzle? Alas, most kids turn off to the razzle-dazzle. Even adults with stepparents admit they are uncomfortable when the new stepparent tries to win their affections. It all backfires on the stepparent who expects to be praised, appreciated, or a little bit thanked for (his) her efforts. When no thanks are forthcoming, the razzle-dazzle turns to bitter-glitter and, pretty soon, plain old ugly resentment. Everyone is worse off than when he started; no one

knows why it didn't work out. For the stepparent with a
tendency to try too hard, to move too quickly, or to expect
too much (anything is too much), there should be a needle-
point pillow with the slogan "Slow Down, You Move Too
Fast," or something equally appropriate. Maybe a printed
hangtag with the instructions:

    1. Did you do your good deed for the day? Fine. Now
you're finished. Lay off.

    2. Channel this energy elsewhere. Isn't there some-
thing you can do for yourself that will give you equal pleasure? (If not, see a shrink.)

    3. Take it back. Don't bake it. Stop making it.

    4. Play hard to get.

    5. Less is more.

    6. To hell with perfection.

Parents are rarely thanked for the good deeds they
bestow upon their children. Stepparents never get thanked.
While the natural parent is prepared for the lack of appreciation he gets—and finds his reward in the child's daily
growth and happiness—the stepparent sees the child only
on occasion and possibly drops everything to make the
stepchild more comfortable . . . expecting thanks but furious when he receives none. It's the stepparent's obligation
to him (her) self to stop extending himself into anything he
doesn't want to do and to stop trying to please.

    Financial. While dating, prospective stepparents sel-
dom see the realities of the financial side of supporting two
families. They see that their would-be mate makes enough
for them to be happy, that their combined incomes satisfy
them, and that all appears to be beautiful. It's only later,
when the difficulties of stepparenting arise and the hurts
and angers of the second family accumulate that the stepparent begins to resent the monies going to support an ex-
wife and numerous children. Of those interviewed for this

book, the most common complaints were "I've taken care of those children, and I know how much they cost, and we pay far too much" and "I don't mind paying for the kids' support, but the money we send goes on his former wife's back." Many second wives have to work to bring in what their husbands pay out. Few families are free from the difficulties of the double load. Studies have shown that families with stepchildren living with them do not begrudge the costs of the children and that stepfathers are usually glad to pay expenses of children that are not theirs. It's paying "x" sum and never seeing where it goes that becomes a matter of contention with the stepparent.

Depending on the divorce settlement, you may or may not be able to beat the financial blues. It's possible you'll have to pay the money and shut up. It's also possible that you can substitute the goods for the the money and supply the receipts for proof of purchase so that you at least know where your money is going. Or that you can renegotiate your payments according to drastic changes in your lifestyle.

How to Avoid The Stepparent Blues

Do not take on responsibility for making the group function as a family. In his search for perfection, the stepparent often enters the family determined to pull it all together and make a go of it. One person valiantly goading the others into obedience and loyalty can provide the semblance of a family. It appears to be a family, but without the efforts of that person everything falls apart. If one person is holding it all together, it isn't much of a family. This is particularly acute in the beginning years of stepparenting when the new parent is out to prove that everyone can live-happily-ever-after and may be trying too hard.

This was a serious problem in our family where I believed (because I also believe in princesses, pirates, dragons, and ghosts) that we should all get together and be a family. My burning enthusiasm drove us to cruise the countryside with constant picnics, visit every museum within driving distance, and walk arm in arm singing camp songs. We had a lot of fun, don't get me wrong. It was great while it lasted. Amy still wistfully asks why we don't go on those family trips anymore. Yet I never had a moment alone, never read one of the trashy novels I keep at my bedside, never sewed all the creations I dreamed of making, and never worked on a weekend assignment. Mike never saw a ball game or did the carpentry he loves. I grew to resent all the familyness I was fostering. I was tired of carrying the ball; I wanted time for myself. When I began to drop out of family activities—trying to send father and daughter off on an outing together—the family trips fell apart. It was no fun without me, said my husband. Translation: he wasn't taking that kid on his own anymore. After some thought I realized that we were only a family when I forced us into it. I bailed out and regained some of myself at the price of a "familyness" we never really had. It was a hard lesson: one parent cannot carry the whole family.

Never take on a task you don't really want to do. Don't take him to the football game because you think it would be nice, or because you should because you're the stepfather. Don't buy her that dress because you feel obligated. If you're doing something you deep-in-your-heart don't want to do, you are going to resent it, particularly if it involves a child who will never thank you for your trouble. Avoid the anger now. Don't do the task. Trade off, find an alternate solution, or go on strike, but don't do anything you don't want to do. You'll be surprised to know that everyone will survive. And you will probably feel a lot better.

Get the competition out of your family. Competition does a lot of good in the right places. Competing with an ex-spouse or the children does no good and lots of harm. If you can't cut it out on your own, see a therapist. Now.

Give yourself rewards. Who cares if it's childish? Every summer that Amy lived with us, I bought myself something wonderful as a reward. I would have preferred if my husband gave me the reward, but he didn't know I had such childish needs. (I was embarrassed to tell. Besides, it doesn't count if you have to ask for it.)

Make a list of the things you hate about being a stepparent or hate about the children. Look at the list twenty-four hours later and decide if each item is valid. Then talk the list over with your mate and set to work on the items that can be changed. Maybe you don't like driving over to her house with him to pick up the kids. Seeing her in that nice home while you scrimp to support her fills you with anger and hate and makes taking care of her children that much more difficult. Solution: don't go. And don't ask about it either. Let it go.

This list making can be particularly valuable to couples who are not yet married. If the list is dismally long and the items are essential ones, perhaps you should rethink this marriage or discover something else to do on your weekends when he has the kids or at least take a hard look at the things you'll have to overcome.

Forget about the distant future and its worries. Take one day at a time. As you—and the children—get older, things will change. There's no need to worry about a lifetime full of misery that may change in a year's time.

Expect nothing. The kids will never let you down if you expect nothing from them. You will never disappoint yourself if you expect nothing.

Must You Love These Children?

Of course not! It's that simple. You don't even have to like these kids. You do have to live with them in a manner non-injurious to your and their health; you do have to make sure they're fed, clothed, and housed. But you don't have to love them and may find freedom in that knowledge.

Usually people plagued by worry fall into one of two categories:

1. *The Liars:* The liars' theme song could well be that old Fred Astaire tune "How Could You Believe Me When I Said I Loved You When You Know I've Been A Liar All My Life?" (Honest, it is a real song. He sang it in *Royal Wedding.*) The liars feel they have to say they love the child (children) even though they really don't. They probably *wish* they did love the kids, but the truth is they don't love them at all and possibly don't even like them. The liars are doing everyone a disservice. They probably aren't deceiving the children, and if they are deceiving their spouse, it's to little avail. 'Fess up now. Be open, honest, and cool. You don't have to like or love the kids. It's okay. All you have to do is be a good parent. And you can be a good parent without telling a child you love him. You can give positive feedback where it's warranted and you feel it. Praise for a job well done, or a favor, maybe a helping hand. If you feel guilty for not telling the child you love him and are tempted to lie to make your case for perfection a better one, you are doing the wrong thing. Besides, few stepchildren believe their stepparents love them anyway . . . especially in the beginning years of a relationship. Love grows over a period of time. Give yourself and the children that time. When you can say "I love you" honestly, it will be worth the wait.

2. *The Nervous Nellies.* The nervous Nellies are too scared to let out their real emotions. They think they have to love the children because it's the right thing to do and they're too nervous to admit to anyone that they hate the kids lest they get in worse trouble. The Nellies are reluctant to tell their spouses they are having a hard time with the kids and usually whip themselves into trying less hard. The nervous need to know it's okay to not love the kids.

It's okay to tell your mate about your hates, fears, and problems with the kids. It's a tremendous benefit to be able to dump your anger on the child's parent (your spouse) without feeling any guilt or worry about the parent's feelings. Dumping your anger on the children is poor form: save it for their parent. But do get it out. And loosen up. Every parent hates his kids at some time or another (often a good bit of the time). It's healthy, safe, and normal to hate the children sometimes. Just because they are children doesn't mean you have to love them or should be embarrassed about not loving them.

I found freedom in a story told to me by one of my friends, herself a stepdaughter. It seems that after her own daughter was born, her father and stepmother came to visit the baby. Laden with gorgeous dresses and wonderful presents, the stepmother—who had been married to my friend's father for about twenty years—was anxious to be a good grandmother. "I saw for the first time that she really was a nice lady and wanted to be part of the family," said my friend, "and I felt sorry for how we treated her all these years. But it made me hate her more knowing how unfair I'd been to her. I've hated her since I was a child and I will always hate her. It's not her fault, but I have no room to like her in my heart." This was from a grown, otherwise rational woman. I saw through her story that no matter what I did, Amy would always blame some things on me because I was the intruder. That realization gave me a tremendous freedom to stop loving her. While I've never been able to totally unlove her, I have been able to let go some and for the first time see the value of not loving the stepchildren.

In fact, there is a lot to be said for not loving the children. A large percentage of the stepparents interviewed reported that their biggest problems came from loving, extending themselves too far, giving too much, and showing feelings that were not returned or appreciated. Those who "treated my stepchild as if he (she) were my own" had the most regrets.

So if you don't love the children, or they don't love you, slow down. Examine these points and see if they help you:

• You don't have to love anyone you don't want to love.

• Love can grow. Often love comes with time, patience, and understanding.

• You don't have to love someone back. A child may tell you he (she) loves you, putting you on the spot—or so you think. The child may be a liar or a nervous Nellie and not mean what he (she) is saying. He might be trying to manipulate you, or he may genuinely mean it. Either way, you don't have to tell someone you love him because he told you the same thing. Love need not be mutual.

• Love-hate is common in all families and very common in steprelationships. No one loves his children all the time. It's normal, healthy and should be expected.

• You may not love in December as you did in May. Relationships with stepchildren lack the continuity of natural child-parent relationships. There are a lot more ups and downs with step-families, and a lot more opportunity to get rid of the kids if they misbehave or are out of favor. Natural parents rarely kick the kids out of the house when they come to a difficult time; they work it out. In divorced families, natural and stepparents may choose the easy way out by shipping the kids to another parent. This can change your affections quickly.

• Don't lie about whom you love and why. Remember what happened to Pinocchio.

3.
Nitty-Gritty
Stepparent

The First Morning

I didn't know any better. It was that simple. I thought being a parent, even a stepparent, was a natural continuation of my own being. I would be everything I was, and more. I expected to wake up in the morning and be my same old self, a working woman, who coincidentally had the care of a seven-year-old child under control. I never considered that a parent lives in an entirely different part of the real world and that I would never again be able to buy a dress without wondering if ice cream would wash out of it.

I learned the desperation of my situation in a mere twenty-four hours. The first day of parenting was all it took. I may be slow, but I knew my life had changed after just one day. The first day of parenthood I felt like I was hit by a truck. Granted, I have never been run over by a truck, but I do have a very good imagination, and if the truth be told, on my first day of motherhood I prayed to be run over by a truck. Gently, of course.

It was dark when I left my office and wandered toward the grocery store, trying to remember if it was Captain Crunch she wouldn't eat or Alphabits she had to have. I soon found myself eyeing medium-sized trucks and fantasizing the accident. The truck would be a light one (preferably ten pounds) and I would be merely dented, nothing serious, but scrunched up enough to end up in an elegant (that means not painted green) hospital room (which my insurance would pay for) where I could wear a fancy nightgown and sit in the middle of the bed reading magazines. My meals would be brought to me and my sleep guaranteed. My appearance would be excused and I'd be free to watch game shows whenever I felt like it. My stepdaughter would not be allowed to climb in bed with me—or even to visit, better yet—and I would have some time alone with her father ... my husband.

It was a great fantasy. But I was saddled with reality. There would be no hospital room or fancy nightgown or uninterrupted meals. Instead, it was like this:

At 6:30 in the morning she bounced into our bed and crawled between my husband and me. (We are now forced to wear pajamas.) After tossing and turning, pulling all the covers off of me in an attempt at a cuddle-huddle, we decided more sleep was out of the question.

Because I am the mother, the smaller details of getting up come into my domain. I stagger out of bed, shouting "up, up, everybody up" and then go into a rendition of "rise and shine and give God your glory, glory" which is very garbled because I am trying to brush my teeth while singing. I put toothpaste on everyone else's toothbrush—a ritual

my husband and I have reserved from our first morning together—which I mention now only because in fifteen minutes I will ask my stepdaughter if she has brushed her teeth.
She will assure me that she has, and I will return to the
bathroom on some other errand only to find her toothbrush—completely as I left it, toothpaste and all—sitting
neatly on the sink.

The two of us will then proceed to make breakfast—something I never do under normal circumstances because I get a doughnut and milk in the shop across the
street from my office. But, alas, we are a family now, and
it's important for families to eat meals together, and besides, we have a growing child and children must eat good
breakfasts to grow up healthy and strong—or so my mother
always told me. (And if you don't eat the crusts of the bread
you won't have curly hair.) My stepdaughter will punctuate
the breakfast preparations with a continuous monologue on
how to do whatever it is I am doing. After all, she tells me,
her mother won a French toast contest. I mean, who ever
even heard of a French toast contest?

She sets the table. But she does a messy job and the
silverware is not placed in any direct relationship to the
place mat or the person who is supposed to use it. I am an
aware mother (even though I've only been at it one hour),
so I see immediately that I am in a terrible bind. Do I praise
her efforts, knowing that praise is what makes the world go
'round and leave it at that, knowing that in the true relationship of the silverware to her education and our future
relationship no one really gives a damn how she sets the table, or do I firmly instruct her in the proper way to set the
table (though I myself don't know if I believe in "proper")
and explain to her that this is my house and this is the way
things will be done? An important psychological drama is
unfolding in my very own kitchen and I haven't even had a
cup of coffee yet.

Finally, we are ready to eat. She pours too much syrup on her French toast and complains that it's too soggy to eat. She refuses to drink her juice because it didn't come in one of those little cans like her mommy buys. Eventually, (has it only been twenty minutes?) she will help me clear the table. She is desperate to be helpful. I am appreciative but wary: her help costs me time and effort. Now I must stand by watching what she does to make sure we lose no forks to the garbage bag while acting busy to make her think I'm not spying on her or suspicious of her every awkward move. I could have done it myself but I am being patient because she is Learning Something and Contributing to the Family Relationship. Can I take much more?

She dresses herself and picks out the worst combination imaginable. I decide that it's better for her to find her own way and make some mistakes than to force my own judgment and fashion sense on her. It takes tremendous energy to keep my mouth shut because I know that later in the day she will come to my office where I am employed as a fashion expert, and everyone will see her in this awful outfit and reconsider my position. Nevertheless, I keep my mouth shut because choosing one's own clothes is a Growing Experience. And I am an aware mother. I braid her hair while grilling her on the whereabouts of my shoes and scarf she last wrapped around her Snoopy in a weak attempt at chic. I am exhausted . . . and still undressed.

In a hurry now (my first day of parenthood has used up 'way more time than I scheduled) I go for my briefcase only to find it is now part of a fortress. Amy thinks I should leave my briefcase home today so she can continue playing in her fortress. Near tears she tells me she even wants to take a picture of it for her mommy. I think I hate her. And it's only nine o'clock in the morning.

Rejection

No one has to deal with rejection on a more continual basis than the stepparent. The unencouraged lover will finally get the message and cast around for the "other fish in the sea," but the stepparent is trapped, enduring any number of insults. For the stepparent, rejection is an everyday occurrence.

I thought I was well equipped to handle rejection. I have been a free-lance writer for over two years. Daily the mails bring rejections. Personal letters. Form letters. Even telexes delivered right to my desk. So used to rejections am I that I no longer have the need to reconsider the intelligence of a rejector while wadding up his meager message that once meant hope and throwing it against the upholstered walls of my office in sputtering rage. I am immune to rejection.

I am immune to rejection except from my husband's daughter. Rejection from Amy turns a sunny day black, a full heart empty. It ruins my cuticles, empties my stomach, and demolishes my appetite. Amy matters to me. My success as a stepparent matters. And her rejection—or her mother's rejection—are the knives they fight their nastiest duels with.

Mine is a common dilemma, say the experts. Most stepparents care too much and are therefore too vulnerable to rejection. No one, no one at all, likes to get kicked in the teeth . . . especially with any consistency.

Rather than letting hurt feelings suffered through rejection turn into anger, and more misery for the entire family, there are some ways to protect yourself:

- Before you even become a stepparent, face up to facts realistically. Be aware that you are in for a lot of rejection.
- Drop your fantasies about what a good stepparent

you will be and how much the children will love you. You are setting yourself up.

• Don't care about the relationship so much, or the children so much. Keep reminding yourself that not only are they not your children, but they never will be. (Unless you plan adoption.)

• Look for areas of conflict from which rejection can stem so you are better prepared to deal with it.

• If rejection is imminent, don't let them know they hurt you. Rejection is a forceful weapon. They are out to hurt you.

• Act like you don't care. Always live your life for yourself and your marriage.

• Be prepared to give them a break. Don't reject them to get even just when they're ready to give you a chance.

Custody

I liked being Amy's mother. Although I was often delighted to see her leave, I immediately found that I missed her. When we were reunited, it seemed we should have always been together. I began to ask my husband if we could get custody. If not custody, then joint custody. If not joint custody, could Amy come live with us for a school year as if she were a foreign exchange student? Mike sadly said that none of these things were possible.

He was wrong.

While we were not willing to put up the legal fees and emotional expenses involved in pursuing the matter, custody arrangements can be changed. We felt that as much as we would like to have more of Amy, her mother was an excellent mother and any trouble we made now would be with us for the rest of our lives. The situation was working; why tamper with it?

Yet because my husband was divorced in a time when mothers automatically got custody of their children and lawyers didn't even know to advise fathers to seek joint custody, my husband and I are at the mercy of Nancee Simmons' whims and ways of life. It she's too busy to take Amy, we get the child more often! If she is feeling jealous or overprotective, we can't see Amy. Should an argument arise, Nancee has the ultimate weapon: you cannot see Amy anymore. Fathers (or parents) who do not have joint custody have no say in their child's well-being or even when they can see their children. (That's one of the reasons some parents are moved to kidnapping.) The children are pawns in a game no one wins.

If you do not have joint custody at the time of your divorce and now seek it, you're going to have to have the cooperation of your ex-spouse or an excellent reason for your change of mind and why you didn't take joint custody in the beginning. A very good reason. Talk to your lawyer about it, and your ex-spouse. Don't try to surprise anyone with a guess-what-I'm-going-to-do attempt. The custodial parent is at the advantage, so take it easy.

Now then, if the custodial parent won't let you see your kids on court-appointed days or holidays, you can go to court and get an order in your favor. That doesn't mean you can make the custodial parent hand over the kids. While the law backs you up, it does not sanctify kidnapping. If you don't have joint custody and you take the kids, you can get slapped with a kidnapping rap—which is a felony. If you have joint custody, no kidnapping rap.

Custody can, of course, be shifted from one parent to another without any legal hassles—or negotiations. Often a custodial parent can't handle the care and support of the children and freely turns custody over to the noncustodial parent. If you are the accepting parent, it is wise to get at least a letter of agreement stating the intent and purposes of the transfer so you can be protected at a later date. (Once you act in *loco parentis* for any period of time, the court will probably find you the legal parent.)

Okay, try this one. Father and stepmother have custody of father's two children because their natural mother is declared unfit. Father is killed in a car accident. Stepmother, who has given these children the only stable home they have known, is challenged by the parents of the natural mother who now want custody of the grandchildren claiming that blood is thicker than water, or whatever else they want to claim. If stepmother was smart enough to adopt these children, which she has every legal right to do, she is okay—the kids stay with her. If not, she could very well lose the kids—depends on the judge and the surrounding circumstances.

Maybe a more simple case: you live in a different state from the children and operate under a specific set of custody laws. You move back to the same state as the children. Your former spouse wants to stick to the agreement as adjudicated. You want to see the kids every other weekend. If you have joint custody, you have no problem. If you don't, you go to court. You will probably win, unless there are reasons why you shouldn't see the children more often.

It's getting more and more common for the judge to ask the children which parent or what arrangements they prefer. Fathers are being awarded custody certainly not in an equal number of cases, but with serious regularity. It is socially acceptable for children to not live with their natural mother, so fathers and children are getting more to say, and do, in the making of custody agreements.

Obviously, the best custody agreement is joint custody (assuming that both parents are equally capable of raising the children). In lieu of joint custody, you should know that your arrangements can be renegotiated—just as child support can be renegotiated—under the proper circumstances.

Dealing With The Ex-Spouse

Unless you are one of the small percentage of adults who marry single parents, you have married someone who had children with a different spouse or, to be more modern about it, mate. (They might not have been married!) Whether those children were adopted, planned, prayed for, or complete accidents, they now exist. They will rarely go away just because you wish they would. Marrying a person with children from a former marriage means not only getting some new children, but getting a new former spouse, who will definitely be part of your new family.

It is quite possible to have former husbands and wives completely disappear, never to be rediscovered. This is never possible when children are involved. When there are kids, no amount of magic can make the ex-spouse disappear. We suddenly find that we're all in this marriage together, for better or for worse. So learning to deal with his ex-wife or her ex-husband is going to be an important part of stepparenting and matrimonial survival.

I discovered I was to be a second wife and stepmother on my second date with my husband. We had just decided to get married and were confessing the details of our past lives we thought appropriate to air. We compared salaries, magazine subscriptions, ideal vacation spots, and future goals. Since my husband was thirty-five, I was relieved he had a former wife and child. (It always made me nervous to consider a previously unmarried thirty-five-year-old man.) I immediately vowed to handle the former wife and child in a civilized and sophisticated manner, becoming my high intelligence. I knew she was prettier than I, richer, more elegant, and possessed of curves I've never known. But I knew I was smarter. It was some comfort. Besides, we all lived three thousand miles apart, we swore we could never live any place but New York City (so much for swearing), and friendships can be taken a lot more seriously at great distances.

My husband's first wife, Nancee Simmons Barrington Grant, came from an old southern family, where everyone was called by his or her double name. Hence Nancee Simmons. She was born gorgeous and remained that way all her life. (I was born gorgeous and turned at age three.) Her light blonde hair never turned mousy, her fingernails never broke, and her nose never needed fixing. She went to a fancy college, speaks French fluently, and is completely at home with a butler, chauffeur, and personal maid to draw her bath. While my maid barely speaks English, Nancee's is English. She (Nancee, not the maid) has been married three times (my husband was number two, a few years after a teenage marriage ended in annulment), and now lives with unofficial number four. She is noted in the society columns almost daily and signs her checks with her full name, Grant being the name of her most recent husband, the penniless movie star. She's a warm, gracious woman, who didn't mind marrying men with no money or family pedigree. She's a terrific mother and is probably the kind of woman you'd meet at a cocktail party and decide to have lunch with. Alas, she and my husband came from such entirely different backgrounds that the marriage was doomed before it began.

Nancee married my husband to scandalize her family (which she did), and Mike married Nancee to scandalize his family (which he did). That was about all they had in common until Amy came along, one year later. The marriage lasted two and a half years. Mike stayed in New York City, Nancee packed the baby and moved to Beverly Hills where her divorced mother lived in great style. You see, Mama Simmons Barrington had left her husband with baby Nancee Simmons many years before, so history was just repeating itself. Clearly, mother and daughter had no use for fathers for their children. Amy, whose real name is Ames Simmons, saw her father only at Christmas and whenever he came to the west coast on business trips. They only reestablished a more serious relationship the year that Mike and I met, when it was agreed that Amy would come to New York and spend two weeks with her daddy in the summer. The two weeks became four when Amy was provided with an instant mother and Mike was spared the ordeal of being a single father.

For the two summers we remained in New York, our relationship with Amy and her mother was friendly. Letters and phone calls went across the country. We moved to California, taking a house next door to Nancee in the spirit of togetherness, wanting to give Amy the benefits of our joint and mutual respect and happiness.

That lasted about three weeks. I then began to hate Nancee Simmons Barrington Grant in a manner I'd never known possible. Unfortunately, no one ever told me it was perfectly healthy to hate your husband's first wife, so I kept these terrible feelings inside me and continued to act as though we were great friends. As the anger and hate mounted, it would spew out in little eruptions. I would get angry at compounded insults or decide to tell Amy exactly what it was her mother was doing that I could do better. I began to dream of murder. It was always Nancee's murder. I would have Nancee killed (or happily do the deed myself), and then Amy could come live with us and the endless conflicts would finally end.

I ended up, ulcer and all, consulting a therapist who encouraged me to shout out my anger—to her, my husband, and Nancee, if it came to that, leaving Amy out of the equation. She allowed that it was stupid for us to have spent family holidays together (Thanksgiving and Christmas at Nancee's home were so much fun?), that I need not be civilized or sophisticated about anything, and that I had merely wasted what was now two and a half years of my life and my marriage by not telling the truth to myself or my husband. The murder fantasies were completely normal ("Jet Set Socialite Dies Mysteriously; film at eleven"), as was my wish to have Amy to myself so I could be the perfect mother.

Always think of yourself first. Think of yourself first, especially when you have no natural children of your own. You are number one and you count. You needn't go into the traditional parental rap about the children coming first with someone else's children. It's not healthy. You come first. Got it?

Consider your priorities. My marriage is top priority. I happened to do it a terrible disservice—and could have ruined it—by not discovering and dealing with my own angers and frustrations and bringing them out into the open. If your mental health and your marriage are top priorities, do what you must to save them.

Isolate your feelings about the ex-spouse and identify them. If it's hate, why do you hate? Get specific. Make a list. Jealousy is a good reason, but find out what you're jealous of.

Deal with your feelings. Only after you have isolated and identified the problems can you begin to deal with them. Is Nancee's figure of any real importance to my life? Of course not. Time to let that one go. I may be forever jealous that she had my husband's child and I did not, but that's something real to be jealous of. Petty jealousies waste energy and just get in the way. You're better off without them.

Consider professional help. There wouldn't be so many books on the market about stepparenting if it were easy to be a stepparent. If your problems with the ex-spouse are working against you and the marriage, maybe it's time for professional help. It could save your marriage.

The Influence Of The Ex-Spouse On Your Marriage

With so many tensions and crosscurrents running through the second family, it makes sense to trace the live wires back to their origins—the first marriage, the old primary family, and the ex-spouse. Of the couples interviewed for this book, a large percentage noted that interference from a previous spouse was the primary cause of marital dysfunction the second time around. Second husbands reported that the first husband was inexorable, either financially, because of his support money to the children, or mentally, because he and his former wife had unfinished business—part of a relationship aside from their children. Women were more jealous of an ex-spouse than men and felt more outright anger, frustration, and distrust. The men considered the former husband to be a problem; women considered the former wife someone to go to war over.

In households where the ex-spouse's remarriage was encouraged, there was considerably less friction within the adult group and therefore more acceptance from the children. "I'm dying for Steve to remarry," said one woman, "he'll be able to give Beth a more stable environment on the weekends and really help me out more." Because this woman will encourage Beth to accept the stepmother and the remarriage of her natural father, all will ease into second familyhood better.

Ex-wives who have not reconciled their feelings toward former spouses, or who have never been able to fully let go, feel jealous of new wives and set up competitive barriers, even while acting like friends. Their children are encouraged to spy on daddy and his new wife, reporting back to mommy who for some reason suddenly fears her own position with her children. Even if a stepmother were a better mother than a natural mother, the children would continue to support their natural mother because of their loyalties to her. Only in cases of death or abandonment do children learn to shift their allegiances.

When there are no children and the influence of a former spouse is felt on the new family, something is very wrong. Get professional help. When children are involved, involvement with the former spouse has to be accepted as the normal way of life. Most people are able to accept the fact that the object of their desires is an adult with children from a previous marriage and cannot be had without those children. Yet few of those same people are willing to accept the ex-spouse and his (her) input as part of their new marriage. Yet as long as there is child support, school, little league, PTA, and Christmas, there is an ex-spouse with a place in your second family. ("I'm getting Amy a stereo for her birthday; why don't you get her some records?")

When I realized I married a child and an ex-debutante as well as a husband, I was stunned. I kept screaming things like "I didn't marry you, I married Amy and Nancee," which was the truth. The first year we were married, Mike hotly denied my argument, claiming that he happened to have a daughter and an ex-wife but that I needn't have anything to do with them. After a few phone calls from Nancee, one or two legal maneuvers, and some tall tales delivered by a young child, Mike conceded that I had a good point. It was impossible to not be affected by Nancee.

In fact, Nancee and I went so far as to publicly admit our relationship and family bond. I call her my ex-wife and she calls me her wife-in-law. Through the care of a child, we are bound to each other for the rest of our lives, (or as long as I am married to her ex-husband). Nancee Simmons, all her good and bad points, are as much my problem—and as much my joy—as they are my husband's. Second marriages are sharing propositions, and it pays to know ahead of time who you're sharing what with.

The immediate family surrounding the first marriage can also influence the second marriage's future. Although these days extended families don't have the power and influence they used to, in some families they should not be looked at askance. In our case, Nancee's mother has been nothing but charming to my husband and me, and has always included us in family events. While she supports Nancee on every matter, she never speaks out against us in front of Amy. There are many grandparents who feel cut away from the family when a divorce ensues and who take the role of a jealous former wife and begin to interfere with their grandchildren and in-laws. "Do you know how difficult it is to have two mothers-in-law?" asked one woman I interviewed. She's got a good point.

The grandparents are usually the last consulted, and the last considered, when divorce occurs. Their hurt feelings, confusion, and bewilderment as to how to treat former in-laws must be dealt with by all members of the family, and their influence on the children and partners in a marriage should not be overlooked.

There are some cases in which the ex-spouse is willing to share the responsibilities of child raising and mother work with the new spouse. This cooperation usually eases matters immensely. Many a child has been confused by friendship between natural parents and stepparent, unable to accept that the real parent doesn't feel threatened or doesn't perceive the stepparent as a wicked witch. Men, more than women, are willing to share their children's upbringing—usually because they are forced to—and stepfathers are shown to be more accepted in families because they participate in a whole family structure. **Sharing** counts.

With this in mind, Nancee and **I tried a system of**

child sharing, or co-parenting, in which we hoped to imitate the natural father-stepfather arrangement so that both of us would have a place in Amy's life and hopefully ease some of the pressures on me. It was fall, and Nancee was extremely busy with her new boyfriend and the social season and a full-time job planning a large charity ball. She had no time for Amy's wardrobe, playtime, and school projects. I was recruited to step in and be the other half of a mother—to do the things that Nancee couldn't do so that together we could provide Amy with a lot of love and a lot of mothering. It appeared to be a great idea and we all took to it enthusiastically. I went to the school play (in the middle of the afternoon, mind you), the classroom Christmas party, and the PTA meetings. I baked for the cake sale, manned a booth for the Christmas carnival, and took Amy shopping for not only her wardrobe, but for Christmas gifts for each member of her mother's family. We deducted the major expenses from Amy's child support, but I was embarrassed to put in for mileage, cake ingredients, or small presents under five dollars. There was an immediate conflict over the monetary arrangement: I was delighted to see where our money was going instead of wondering what Nancee had done with it, but I was angry at the little, but accumulative, expenses that were coming out of my own pocket. Aside from that, the new system seemed to be working. I wanted to be an active part of Amy's life and I got what I asked for. Nancee gave me all the cooperation I could ever ask for. It seemed we had the perfect solution for the stepmothers of the world and would always be a fine example of two women who worked it all out.

We were wrong. While Nancee was completely satisfied with the arrangement (why shouldn't she be, I kept asking myself), I grew more and more miserable. It was a much more demanding job than I ever imagined. Constant changes in my schedule and way of doing business were demanded. I met the changes even though I knew that if or when I had my own child I would not be doing these same things. In order to do the mother work created by being half a mother, I had to give up a lot of my work (that paid the bills) and a lot of my free time. As a result of the new regimen, Nancee had free time on her hands and was getting more and more done. It hardly seemed fair to me. Nancee had conned me into being a glorified baby-sitter or a fancy nanny. I did the crummy jobs and Nancee had her kid whenever she wanted her.

Meanwhile, Amy's attitude toward me never changed. She was her same old adorable self and treated me like the same old baby-sitter she had always treated me as. She was unable to see or appreciate that I was knocking myself out for her and she showed no extra gratitude at all. Naturally, children never know what you're giving up to care for them, and they *expect* you to give them the world, so Amy never thought to show added appreciation. A child's greatest sign of acceptance is when he treats you like part of the family—taking your interest and concern for granted and never saying thank you. And that's why the system fell apart. I not only wanted to be thanked, I wanted to be thanked profusely.

While our child-sharing days marked the height of our cooperation as wife and ex-wife, dissolution of the system and return to an each-woman-for-herself policy backfired. No longer was Nancee willing to cooperate. No longer was I willing to do the things I had been doing as a "good sport." We reached our all-time low. Amy began to carry stories of what her mother had to say about me into our home. I began to insult Nancee in front of Amy. Nancee and I sat down to work it out and found no mutual ground. In the end, I retreated—knowing that the natural mother always wins. Dissatisfied, I began to actively hate both of them.

What Is A Parent, Anyway?

In the good old days a parent was a mommy and a daddy and there was only one to a customer. Today, more and more specialists are telling us that parenting is a verb and he who parents is the parent. This, of course, makes perfect sense to me—because I remember that story we learned in eighth grade science about the baby chimpanzee who was taken from his mother at birth and raised by a chicken-wire-towel-and-robot-mother whom the chimp instantly accepted as the real thing. If the chimp knew the dummy mommy wasn't his own, he never said a word about it to anyone.

Likewise, adoptive parents and stepparents become the parents of record when they perform the jobs of the role. Adopted parents at least start out at the beginning of the child's life and only later tell him he is adopted and perhaps help him to find his natural parents, who will never have a part in the upbringing of the child. In cases of adoption, while there may be more than two parents, there are only two parents of record.

Not so with step-families. With the addition of two stepparents, the Dick and Jane syndrome falls away quickly and we're forced to ask ourselves the most essential of questions: Why not four parents? Who says that two is enough? Or two is right and more is wrong? What about five, or six? If the stepparent were no longer the third (or fourth) wheel, would his position be so precarious and his feelings so easily wounded? Of course not. Why can't a stepparent be more like a parent?

There is always room for another parent in anyone's life. All that's needed is for children, parents, and society to break down their barriers to such an arrangement. Just as they dumped Dick, Jane, and Spot, so must they dump Mommy and Daddy for an inclusive arrangement allowing for Mommy I and Mommy II and Daddy I and Daddy II. Particularly in a time when women seek their freedom from traditional roles and mother work, an additional set of parents can be a boon to any family.

On commenting on the problems of the children of divorce, Margaret Mead blamed American society for fostering the idea that two parents and two parents only support and provide for a child, making him completely dependent on them and no others. When the stepparent, particularly the stepmother, is able to take a place in the family as an equal and integral part of a family relationship, then Cinderella will be revenged.

A parent today, however, is still very different from a stepparent. While custodial stepparents can "parent" and find success and satisfaction, stepparents must often suffer from wanting to parent and not being allowed to do so. One cannot simply announce the intention to parent and live happily ever after. The parent, or stepparent, has to be accepted as such. And therein lies the essence of most of the problems discussed in this book. Stepparenting is usually not parenting.

The Financial Side of Stepparenting

The financial problems of second marriages are serious ones and only the very wealthy can afford to overlook them. When marriages that involve children crumble, who pays for what is an immediate and constant problem that will haunt the partners of the first marriage well into their second, or subsequent, marriages. Unless marrying into one of the great families of fortune, any adult marrying a formerly married person must realize the financial burdens of carrying two households. No matter who works, saves, or contributes to the support of the family, there is always *another* family to support . . . be that an ex-wife who receives a small amount of alimony to set her on her feet, or an ex-wife with three children who is fully dependent on the former husband for maintaining life as known when the couple was happily married.

What the second husband earns is no longer his, but his, hers, and theirs. Many couples consider themselves fortunate when the second wife can work and make back what the husband must pay out to the first wife. Her income is usually thought of as standing clear, or profit, only after the amount paid out is covered. Of the working women interviewed, many expressed bitterness that they are ·living a life-style possible only because they work. As single women their money was theirs alone, as second wives they are working to support two families.

Yet the expense of running two families is one of the last things the about-to-be-married consider. While most people know that two-can't-really-live-as-cheaply-as-one, they never really consider that two families can't live as well as one.

For the instant parents, one of the greatest shocks is the cost of children. The hidden expenses beyond food, clothing, schooling, and camp are usually ignored, until the money goes out and never comes back. Even though the noncustodial parent is probably paying child support, that support does not cover expenses incurred while the children are visiting.

It follows that if child support and doctor bills, as well as weekly visits, are being absorbed by you and your husband, you are giving up something somewhere. Are you that somewhere? How do you feel about that? Speak up now, before it's too late. Is, in fact, your whole style of living going to change because you are marrying a person with children? Will you resent going from the rich, swinging bachelor to the strapped middle-class father? As a single woman, did you blow your paycheck frivolously on the world's most glorious underwear, only now to find out that you don't need one hundred dollar nightgowns and would rather have a maid to help you out with the kids? Even if your logical self tells you it's better to have the help than the nightgown, do you deep down inside resent that you had to make the choice?

To my consternation, I found I was spending a tremendous amount of my own money on my husband's daughter—above the amount he paid out for child support and sometimes without his knowledge. I spent large sums of my own paycheck on Amy as I acquired the buying habits of a grandmother, seeing myself as a cross between the fairy godmother and Santa Claus. I was not trying to buy her love (honest), I was merely buying for her the things I would have wanted for myself. It was never a case of Amy seeing something she wanted and manipulating me to buy it for her. She rarely even went shopping with me. I just discovered the second floor of Saks and my life changed. I found myself seeking out the children's department in every store I wandered into. And I couldn't leave until I'd bought the cutest something they had for sale. I had a constant case of Amy-would-just-love-this.

It took me a long time to realize how much money I was spending and why I got little satisfaction from it. Children, because they are dependent on adults for everything, expect you to bestow the world upon them. Because they expect it, they show little gratitude. No gratitude to a mother may be fine. It's not to a stepmother. Naturally, when the barrage of goodies ended, Amy simply decided I didn't love her anymore and wondered what she had done wrong.

Another area that may bring shocks to the stepparent is the separation or divorce agreement. The new husband (or wife) may be misrepresenting the facts of life without intending to wrong anyone. My husband happens to have the most selective memory in the world. He can't remember his divorce agreement because of the pain involved. So you can imagine the surprise both of us received when we recently found out that Mike had agreed to provide for Amy's college education, many thousands of dollars which must be handed over in cash on her eighteenth birthday. We will have to start saving now in order to meet that clause in the agreement. So before we put aside money for a house of our own or a new car or anything we might want to do for ourselves, we are obligated to stash a little something for Amy's college education. (A sum she gets, by the way, whether she goes to college or not.) It's a good idea to get out the old legal papers and give them a thorough reading before you plan your budget and your mutual finances. There may be a few surprises you hadn't planned.

One of the biggest complaints from noncustodial parents and stepparents is the fact that the law requires them to pay a certain sum but does not require the mother to concede any of the judgmental factors in raising a child to the supporting parent. Many fathers have no say in when they see their children, what school they go to, or what kind of clothes they are bought. Daddy claims he damn well gives the kids enough money to go to camp. The kids return to report that mommy says they can't go to camp because they don't have enough money. Parents who do not have joint custody of their children have little to say for the life-style they are paying for. More than one father has complained, and more than one stepmother has grown bitter, from the financial inequalities alone.

On the other hand, men who marry women with children often complain of their own personal battle: a mental conflict between wanting to be the financial head of the household and the true "daddy" in every sense of the word, resenting that life is dependent on another person paying child support and anger at raising someone else's children—again, the paid baby-sitter syndrome. Even if the stepfather has a happy relationship with his wife's children, it is not uncommon for him to have ego or emotional problems concerning who is paying for what. As much as women's lib has penetrated our daily lives, most men still feel they should be the head of the household and the bigger breadwinner. Inability to casually pay for the additional expenses incurred by a house full of stepchildren can be a serious threat to a man's ego, especially considering that studies show that most stepparents prefer paying for a child living in their own household than one that exists in someone else's family. At what price does the stepparent offer up his former life-style or the things he wants and needs for the benefits of another person's child? And, at what price, does the resentment build a serious block to the marriage and the step-relationship?

What You Can Hope To Accomplish With Someone Else's Children

What you will accomplish with your stepchildren over a period of years depends on a number of factors and has nothing to do with what you *hope* to accomplish when you enter into the step-relationship. When most people enter a step-relationship, especially for the first time, they have tremendous fantasies about what they will accomplish. Besides being the perfect parent, they will make the child into a perfect child and shape his future as if the child were damp clay, just waiting for a stepparent to happen his way.

For success with stepchildren, you can expect one thing and hope to accomplish the same: nothing. As long as you have no expectations, you will do well. You won't pressure the kids to perform what they cannot do. You won't be resentful or angry that they didn't treat you the way they should. You will appreciate their small thoughtfulness and acts of generosity. You will not overpower them trying to impress or persuade. Your feelings are less likely to be hurt. They are more likely to turn to you when they are ready.

- Make no plans for your and their future together.
- Plan to accomplish nothing.
- Have no expectations.
- And the future will be yours.

The Legal Position Of The Stepparent

Reinforcing the fact that stepparents have no real place in their children's lives are the laws, or lack of laws, governing stepparents and their legal relationship with their stepchildren. In most cases, a stepparent has no legal relationship to his (her) kids whatsoever. In the eyes of the law, you may very well be powerless. If you are married to a man with a child from a former marriage and that child lives with you, unless you legally adopt that child you have no legal relationship.

After you have been in *loco parentis* for many years, that is, taking the place of a parent, the court may award you the right to continue in that role. May.

Consult your family lawyer for the best ways of protecting yourself and your family ... but don't get railroaded into any legal agreement you do not favor. An insincere adoption is a terrible mistake for you and the children.

Them Versus Me Syndrome

I know it's preposterous, but I can't help it. It's so ridiculous that I am embarrassed to mention it, but, what the hell. You see, I very often get the feeling that it's Them (the family of the first marriage) against Me. (Mike, Amy, and Nancee against poor, defenseless Suz.) Since Nancee and Mike barely speak to each other now, and when they are speaking it is rarely civil, I know I'm crazy. But the truth is, I often think they're ganging up on me.

Mike and Amy want to go on an all-day family drive. I want to run errands, sew, do my nails, and sit in the middle of the bed petting the cats. I suggest they go without me. Amy says it's no fun without me. Mike says I'm not giving Amy the kind of family attention she needs because she doesn't get it at home. It's simple to me. If Amy were not with us, I could do what I want and Mike could do what he wants. Now, they're ganging up on me. *They* are pressuring *me* . . . two against one.

I say Amy's new room should be blue, Mike says it should be peach, and Amy says she wants red. "And my mommy thinks it should be red, too," she throws in, for good measure. What does Mike know about color and decor, I angrily ask myself? And Nancee? And a now nine-year-old kid? In disgust I throw in the paint chips, tell them to all go to hell and do whatever they damn please. Why did they ask me in the first place?

No matter how small or petty the problem, when the stepparent doesn't feel the support of the family—particularly his mate—his (her) insecurities and frustrations immediately surface. The same rationale that makes children stomp out of the room declaring that no one loves them overcomes the stepparent who is placed in much the same position.

There are a tremendous amount of emotional adjustments that we are forced to make as stepparents, many of which we just aren't ready for. Rejection, especially when it comes from your spouse who is supposed to be on your side, is doubly hard when you feel left out of something created by the first family group.

Indeed, there's so much rejection in being a stepparent that it's only natural that one begins to think the others are ganging up. There are a few ways to beat the syndrome, which will at least turn the tables, even if you inwardly are squirming at your exclusion:

• Act like you have something better to do than be included with them anyway. Then find the something better and go out and do it. I have some of my worst attacks of Them versus Me when my husband and his daughter are doing something musical together. I am tone deaf. I can't even keep time to the music without them staring at me ruefully. I used to feel unloved, rejected, and at war when they plotted their musical adventures expecting me to tag along. Now I go off to the fabric store, buy a few splendid yards, and whip up a creation that will knock them out. Neither has any sewing ability whatsoever. You can go to a movie, visit with a friend, see someone very special, and make the "in" group suddenly feel like they should be doing what you're doing. Let them eat their hearts out.

• You can join in whatever they're doing and be a good sport, refusing to feel as if you don't belong and forcing them to accept you on your own merit. This doesn't usually work when the former first family is reminiscing about the good old days, but if you have strong nerves, you can try.

• Have a secret. I had a boyfriend once who was Machiavellian in deed and thought. He once told me one of

his best tricks: always have a secret. If you don't have a secret, act like you have a secret. Have a secret place, a secret
piece of information, or a secret gift that They can't know
about. Who cares if it's childish?

When you truly feel that they're out to get you, you
have only two recourses: say something about it or shut up.
You may be paranoid; you may be right. Chances are it's a
combination of both.

The Urge to Kill

I know that all parents have times when they would like to
kill their children. I accept it as a fact of life and I'm sure
that it happens even to saintly parents and that maybe even
my mother thought of murdering me. Yet still, I am embarrassed by this confession.

I have often taken pleasure in plotting to kill either
Amy or her mother. Sometimes both of them. And wishing
airplane crashes on a hundred innocent people coincidentally traveling in the same plane as they is not beyond me.

I tell it to you now only at the encouragement of my
friend Susan, who said it was something that had to come
out in the open. Then she confessed that she too is plotting
the murder of her stepchildren, and has prayed for an airplane crash or two.

Then I found out we are not alone.

We are a nation of parents and stepparents, all plotting murder. I have never in my life plotted a serious murder before. I've never wished anyone dead or hated anyone
with sincere passion. Yet I have discovered great satisfaction in working out the gory details of Nancee's dismember-
ment. I only come to my senses when I realize the after-

math of my wretched excess. What will it profit me if I am
in jail?

My husband, quite naturally, is horrified that I admit
to such fantasies and wants to believe I'm teasing. He refuses to listen to the details, will not be my confessor, or
serve as my accessory. He led me to believe that I was
slightly psychotic for having these thoughts and that they
certainly were bad thoughts. It was only Susan who freed
me. If she too had the same fantasies, then all stepparents
must be suffering the same agonies.

I have been assured by my therapist that fantasy is a
good way of working out problems and, as long as I stay
within the world of fantasy, I am harming no one and possibly doing a lot of good. I found that immensely comforting.

Further talks with Susan have proved that not only
do we dream of a world free of ex-wives or stepchildren,
but that we are attracted to the same kinds of crimes. This
possibly is because we are such good friends that by now
we think alike, but it seems more to have to do with the pa-
thology of anger. We both visualize beating, bludgeoning,
or stabbing deaths. (Colonel Mustard in the Kitchen with
the Wrench.) An overdose of barbiturates would never satisfy us. The imagined act of the murder gives pleasure in
the release of anger through repeated striking motions. The
fantasy holds up only if the murder involves pain or tor-
ture, blood or bleach. Death by speeding car is unsatisfac-
tory. A tornado will never swoop down and pluck up only
one—as it did Dorothy. A plane crash has its advantages because I could always claim it wasn't my fault and live the
rest of my life guilt free. Also acts of God leave one genuinely guilt free. But they're not much fun. The murders Susan and I are planning are actually freeing our spirits and
beating out all our hurt feelings and hidden anxieties.

I am desperately afraid that confession of these
thoughts will lead Nancee to decide she can't leave her

child in my safekeeping, the exact reason she has been looking for to deny us Amy's presence, and that she will never reveal that deep in her soul, she too is planning Amy's demise.

Lest anyone take my plans too seriously, I consulted a shrink who calmed my fears by saying that my fantasizing is very common among stepmothers and that the usual object of our hatred is the natural mother. The complete fantasy is that the stepmother kills the natural mother and gets custody of the stepchildren because she (the stepmother) can care for them better than the natural mother. What a relief. Now Nancee needn't fear for Amy's safety—just her own.

If you too are plotting to kill, sit back and relax. Plot away. It's really okay. If the plot moves out of your fantasy world and into your real world, seek professional help. Otherwise just remember that it's not illegal to think of a crime. It's only against the law when you do it. (It is illegal to plot to overthrow the government—but you can plot anything else to your heart's desire.)

Sex And The Stepparent

The addition of a child—or children—to your family will immediately change your sex life for the worse. Naturally, the addition of a baby to your household also changes your sex life. But it's a change you are more or less expecting and we grow with the changes.

In an instant step-family, one suddenly finds himself confronted with a lack of privacy. The two of you were used to being alone. If she had kids, she left them at home with the baby-sitter while she rendezvoused at his place, or a nearby motel. If he had kids, it was only occasionally on weekends. Suddenly you are married and reality sets in. You're not alone in the house. You're self-conscious about being seen naked by strangers, you resent having to get dressed when you preferred to be naked, having to grab a robe to get the newspaper or water the plants. Your once uninhibited sounds of pleasure may now be heard by the little monsters—even wake them up. A rendezvous on the kitchen floor, under the dining room table, or against the sewing room wall is now out of the question. (While the Total Woman makes suggestions for trying out new locales, she doesn't say what to do with the kids who may wander by.)

Mike and I first lived in an apartment with its only bathroom adjoining our bedroom. Need I tell you how many times Amy would barge through our bedroom to get a drink of water? She slept in the living room, one thin wall away, and I suddenly found myself terribly uncomfortable and unsexy.

Instant parents may also find no time for sex. Although time and privacy are very much related when it comes to sex, there are also fewer hours in the day when one has no children to care for. This is true for all parents, not just stepparents, and particularly true for working mothers and stepmothers. The first summer I was a mother I fell asleep nightly before Amy. I was too exhausted to even consider sex.

You can try to protect your sexual relationship by taking a few precautions:

• Have a separate room for the children. Don't put them in the same room as you and your mate. I hope their bedroom won't even be next door to your bedroom. Make sure that the kids needn't enter your bedroom for any reason (to gain access to the bathroom, etc.).

• Make it known that you must have time to yourselves. Post "No Visiting" hours. Get a "Do Not Disturb"

sign from a hotel, and teach the kids to respect it. Make a
"Go Away" sign.

• Farm out the kids occasionally. Send them to
grandparents, friends, or relatives on overnights. They'll
think it's a big treat and so will you. Or hire a baby-sitter
and go to a hotel for the night. You'll be glad you got away.

• If you're angry, speak up. Buried anger can ruin
your sex life.

Remember not to flaunt your sexuality. It will offend
children of all ages, and may create serious trouble with
teenagers. Also remember that while incest is common in
stepfamilies, it is not healthy.

The Jennifer Solution

Stepmotherhood made me discover that I loved motherhood. Once Amy became part of my life, I was hooked. I
never again thought of myself as a childless adult. I always
considered myself a parent.

When I discovered that a major fault in our relationship was my giving too much, I was in a terrible bind. I
couldn't not be myself, could I? It would leave me bereaved
and brokenhearted to not buy her that little dish that
matched her room so perfectly, or that cute book about the
pink crocodile. It was depressing to think I had to be cool
and standoffish and refrain from gift giving and craft making when my real nature is just the opposite.

So I found Jennifer. Jennifer is the same age as Amy
and is the daughter of one of my best friends. Jennifer's
mother is also of the hugging and kissing and giving and
loving school of motherhood, and she has never felt at all
threatened in her position as Jenny's mother. So she lets

me borrow Jennifer to get my mothering out of my system. Everything that I buy for Amy goes to Jennifer now, everything that I make now hangs in Jenny's closet. Jennifer thinks I'm terrific, and is wildly appreciative of my efforts. Jennifer's mother loves it and often leaves the child in my care.

It makes me sad and hurt to think I cannot give Amy all of the things I would like to. Her mother has pressured her to not accept anything from me, tangible or intangible. And our relationship is stronger when I don't give as much as I would like to. Being cool is a talent I have never acquired. Certainly trying too hard is a problem all stepparents have, though I have never considered myself to be in this category. My instincts to go overboard come quite naturally.

If you have the same problem and find it harmful to your step-relationship, you may do well to consider finding another child who can appreciate you. There are friends' children, neighborhood children, and plenty of needy children. You may have to live with the rejection of your stepchildren, but there is a child out there who is waiting to meet you. Honest.

4.
Part-time Parenting

The Occasional Parent

Obviously, I became a stepparent thinking I had become a mother. In fact, I was a bit smug about it. I'd neither conceived, ruined my figure, nursed, nor toilet trained this child—she had not spit up on me, ruined my weekend with measles, thrown food from her hot tray, nor written on my walls with magic marker. I thought I'd made a clever little deal.

Amy needed a mother; I liked being her mother. Who could ask for anything more? Well, we did. We moved to Los Angeles, saying gleefully how much fun it would be to see Amy more often.

I made lists of the things we would all do together:
1. Go to PTA meetings.

2. Go camping in Yosemite.

3. Have a Halloween party for the whole school class.

The list went on to twenty-seven variations of the above. We were planning on being very involved with our daughter.

So we moved to Los Angeles, gave up summer parenting, and began every-other-weekend-parenting with in-between visits for the mutual convenience of the two sets of parents who at that time cared about each other's convenience.

Motherhood suddenly lost its pizzazz. I quickly decided I was a baby-sitter, not a mother. I was right, of course, but that didn't make it any better. Amy's mother decided that Amy just didn't need two mothers. If you think about it rationally (who wants to be rational?), any mother may well react the way Amy's did: she was threatened by the mom from the East. In the same situation, I might feel the same way. Who knows? Nancee was too much of a politician to come straight out and ask me to duel. She played a cooperation game. She gave me a part in Amy's life. I was allowed to drive car pool, pick Amy up from school and take her to her guitar lesson, wrap birthday presents, and sew Amy's hems.

After a few months of this nonsense I suddenly realized that being a full-time-part-time mother in the summer was entirely different from living in the same town and being an every-other-weekend-sometimes-more mother. And the more I checked within my group of stepmother friends, the more their stories varied depending on the custodial arrangements and how they adjusted to them.

I'd been a perfectly happy summer mother. I turned into a perfectly wretched weekend mother. So miserable was I that we tried several variations of custody to make things easier for me—and thus the rest of us.

The You-Call-Us-We'll-Call-You Custody Arrangement. In this arrangement each of the parties (Amy in one corner in the green trunks; Mike and Suzy in the soggy blue bathrobes in the other corner) decided there would be no formal custody arrangements and because we were all so friendly, we would just pick up the telephone and say "Hey, how about dinner tomorrow night?" or "Can I come visit next weekend?" or something civilized along those easy-to-understand, easy-to-handle lines. It didn't work. The phone never rang. I finally asked my office to put through my business calls just to hear the sound of the phone. But there was never any kid's voice saying, "Hey dad, can I come play?" Naturally, because Amy didn't call us we were hurt, so we didn't call her. We couldn't take the rejection. We did call once. We were putting up the Christmas tree, a family pride, and we both agreed that Amy would love to see it. I goaded Mike into calling her, to invite her for dinner, to look at the tree, and to get her present. I certainly didn't think she'd turn down the present part. She did. She said she'd have to ask her mommy if she felt like visiting us and my husband hung up the phone in tears.

The Why-Hire-A-Baby-sitter Custody Arrangement. Nancee has a very full social calendar. We decided that since we all lived so close to each other, she shouldn't waste money (our money) on a baby-sitter. Amy would stay with us and we would have more chance to see her as a normal kid, help her with her homework, and do the things real parents do rather than be just weekend parents. We even had family slumber parties in which everyone giggled a lot and had a great time, except Mike who complained that Amy tossed around so much in her sleeping bag that it kept him awake all night. So Amy got her own room which we decorated in pink and flowered chintz and filled with a lot of her spare toys and gave her notches that were fitted to her height for her clothes and always kept clean underwear in the drawers. From our point of view, this was a fairly successful arrangement. Nancee, however, who was out almost every night, realized that her kid was beginning to live with *us* and visit with *her*. I even wanted to push for custody. Nancee promptly replaced us with a sixteen-year-old girl, and that was the end of that.

The After-School-Quick-Little-Visit Arrangement. Since Amy was finished with school at three and wasn't picked up until five (by the sixteen-year-old baby-sitter), we tried an arrangement whereby I sneaked into the schoolyard to visit with Amy or took her off to run some errands and visit with me and, if her father could get off from work, with him too. Mostly we hung out at the local grocery store and I bought her a yogurt push-up (raspberry). This wasn't particularly convenient and it took a big hunk out of my day's schedule. It would have been great for a stay-home mommy, but it didn't work out too well for me. Besides, my husband didn't get much out of this arrangement and Amy is his child.

The Father-And-Daughter-Alone Arrangement. I really hated this one, but in the midst of my hating Amy more, I would send Mike out for a day to take her on his own. She claimed she never got a chance to have her daddy to herself, which was true, and while I hated being cut out and thought she was a real brat for making a big to-do about getting us apart, it was a way of not seeing her when I didn't want to. It flopped. Mike hated her those days, too.

The I-Never-Want-To-See-You-Again Arrangement. Worked great, but we started to miss her and gave in after six months. Returned to the original *Full-Time-Part-Time Arrangement* in which we played like we lived in New York even though we lived around the corner. We would prefer custody ourselves, but that doesn't seem too realistic a proposition so we are resigned to our miserable fate: secondary families are part-time families and each part-time family has its own set of realities.

Why Stepmothers Are More Miserable Than Stepfathers

There are very few stepfathers who marry noncustodial parents. While women are giving joint custody or total custody to their ex-husbands more than ever before, the majority of divorced women keep their kids. Most stepfathers become stepfathers by marrying women with children from a previous marriage who have those same children living with them. So stepdaddy moves in and whammo has a place to be and a new family. He adjusts or moves out. Even on weekends, which may resemble a Marx Brothers comedy of opening, shutting, and revolving doors as children come, go, and rotate fathers, the stepfather usually has a regular place in his new family. He doesn't have as much to worry about.

It's the noncustodial parents who are constantly rearranging their lives to meet custody agreements. It's the stepmothers and future stepmothers who have the burden of the inconsistencies of life.

Women also, more than men, fantasize about what good mothers they will be. Men, for the most part, accept what society has dealt them: they are not "good with children," their fathering role is secondary and supportive rather than primary. It is the women, the ones who are groomed for motherhood from infancy, who believe that they will walk in, cook a nice pot roast, and make everything okay. Women think mothering is their "thing," they can do it with their eyes closed—as if it were built into the genes, an instinct rather than a learned skill. So women automatically get ready to take a role in the lives of their husband's and date's children. And women are more miserable because of it. When you're left out, you have a right to be miserable.

I'm Just His Date

Despite what mother said about nice men not getting divorced, it's getting more and more difficult to find any man—nice is extra—who hasn't been married before. Of those formerly married men, sixty percent have children from a former union. (Look for the union label—it probably means you'll be a stepparent.) Likewise, all those divorced men you are dating were once married to women (we assume) who are now out there glutting the singles' market and making the competition more stiff. Statistics show that fifty percent of the formerly married men marry women who have never been married before and who have no children. But their ex-wives will also remarry, creating more stepfathers.

Dating a parent is different from dating a nonparent. And if you think dating is different, then just consider how different marriage will be. Both men and women in the dating and remarriage market are finding difficulties.

Children are often considered a liability. No one really wants to become a stepparent, especially when the natural parents are alive. The formerly married are often concerned about a date's reaction to the fact he (she) has children. He (she) often fears it makes him (her) a lot less attractive . . . unless the date is Florence Henderson. While most divorced adults quickly agree that "if he (she) doesn't accept me with children, he (she) is not the one for me," it sometimes takes a while to get to this stage. Women often choose to hide their kids and men just don't mention their weekend obligations. Many admit there are children, but stay hazy on the details until they know if it will matter or not.

Children may demand separate but equal dating conditions. Women who are trying to protect their children from their social lives and would rather the kids not see men coming in and out of mother's life, usually must endure assorted inconveniences to keep the children and dates separate but equal. Dates are often met out, rather than at home. Weekends out of town are arranged around a sitter and a lie to the kids. Many men find it very demeaning to be treated like a college kid on a weekend binge from the dormitory, and want to know why they can't meet the kids. In fact, they always want to know why until they do finally meet them.

Children are a responsibility. Whether your date sees his children once a year, every weekend, or lives with them, he (she) is always aware of their existence and of some obligation to them. A single couple may blithely walk by a toy store and never even know they passed it by. A parent sees the toy store, shops the windows, and makes a mental note of association with one or all of his (her) children. I have found that rarely a day in my life goes by that I don't think of Amy at least once. I am very aware of her as an individual person, with likes and dislikes. I constantly see little things I want to buy, tell her about, or take home and share with her. Few parents can eliminate the memory of their child's personality from the reality of their everyday doings, so childless adults should be aware that even the most disinterested or uninvolved parents have a frame of reference that childless people rarely have.

Children are expensive. We all know that—and as inflation rises, children become more and more expensive. Women with children, unless left in fabulously wealthy circumstances, are well aware of the monetary threat their children pose to them in the dating market. A woman who receives alimony will no longer get it when she remarries. Marriage may actually cost her bucks. Men with children of their own are often looking at supporting not only a second wife, but the extra expenses of that woman's children not provided for by her child-support payments. Even casual dating is more frightening when children are involved. When he decides to take her and her two kids to dinner and the movies, the bill is quite possibly double what it would have been if she were single. The price of dinner for four at a family restaurant would make a memorable dinner for two someplace else.

Children change your life-style. The little buggers happen to get in the way. Whether pleasantly or not, the kids are always there. Picture that romantic vacation the two of you have been planning: ten days to roam the French wine country in a convertible roadster stopping at the quaint chateaux and living it up. Now picture it with a kid or two along. Not the same, is it? Vacations will change, leisure time will change, solitary time will change—life will change when there are children involved. No matter how solitary, private, and romantic the courtship may be, there will be weekends, months, or holidays when the world will change rapidly: the day the kids come to visit. Even if you only have one child, one day of the year, that one day will be different. Very different. No reason to act surprised when it happens.

Now then, if you are dating a parent, you should know that only three kinds of people introduce their dates to their children: (1) the crazies, (2) the selfish, and (3) the serious.

The Crazies. The crazies you can usually spot right out in the open. They're probably just divorced, sore, and totally unable to cope. They want you—the date—to parent them, as well as their children. The crazies don't care how many meaningless relationships they expose their children to, or what sort of relationships develop between the kids and the dates, because, well, they're crazy. Before you drop a crazy, remember that this could just be a phase and time, therapy, and lots of talk may work it all out. Maybe.

The Selfish. There's no hope for the selfish because they will always be selfish. If you want to have a relationship with someone who's selfish, that's your problem, just don't forget that I warned you. (Here's my mother's trick for telling if he's selfish. Buy a large steak and have him carve. If he gives you the best piece (with the eye), he's your man. If he takes the best part for himself, dump him.) The selfish parent wants to supply his (her) kids with the joys of a stand-in parent. Women with sons often seek out dates to serve as role models for their boys. Fathers might require a "feminine touch" for a family outing . . . and guess who gets to be feminine? The selfish do have a sneaky racket going for them. Their children are usually adorable and we fall into their trap, thinking how much fun it is to play mommy or daddy for a day, weekend, and maybe forever . . . and not being so unselfish ourselves, we may decide to use the kids as a way to our own ends. Many a parent has been made through proper use of his kid. (Remember what mother told you about the way to a man's heart being through his stomach? Forget it. It's through his kids.) Many a date has tried to manipulate a possible mate through his children. (Ugh, those hockey games!) It usually doesn't work out too well in the end, though, because both parties are too selfish to face the rigors of what they have wrought.

The Serious. The serious contender decides the time to meet the children is after your relationship has been clearly defined and some sort of permanence agreed on. Few people want their children to become attached to someone they are not planning a long-term relationship with, nor do they want the kids entangled in their dating/sexual lives until the time is propitious. It used to be (in the good old days) that he (she) invited you home to meet mom and dad and you knew it was serious. This is the same thing. Only nowadays you go home to meet the kids. Once a serious relationship is established, it is certainly time to meet the kids. Warning: if you think it's serious and he (she) still doesn't want you to meet the kids, something is wrong. Find out what today.

Engaged Versus Married

Both adults and children often complain that things were different before the wedding, as if they were better. The children knew the prospective stepparent, there is no change in life-style, nothing appears to be different—yet it's *different*. And different isn't good.

Even to adults who have lived together for years, there's something a little bit different about being married. When children are involved, that difference magnifies itself. You may never have been considered an outsider or intruder until the day you got married. Then suddenly, whammo, trouble right here in River City.

What happened was simple. Only with your wedding did the children realize that their parents were divorced and were never going to get back together again. Every child of divorce harbors a secret fantasy that mom and dad will go back together. Even if mom or dad is dating someone else, they hope the natural parents will reunite. When one of those partners marries someone else, the dream is over. Then the child must face the truth about the divorce and his new life. Competition with the stepparent, which may have been formerly kept to a minimum, is now strong. This is for real. The child is fighting for his identity in his parent's eyes—even though the parent rarely views the child differently, the child doesn't understand this. "You love him (her) better" is the usual response that brings on all the trouble.

When Amy spent her first month with us, Mike and I were engaged. Because we were functioning as a family unit (or trying our best to), we found it best to face the outside world as a real family. We wore our wedding rings and called each other husband and wife, with Amy as daughter.

One of the best advantages of this was that I never had to shift my position in the family. I didn't come in as a date and get elevated to a mother. I started with the exalted rank of mother. We were determined to show no difference between our engagement period and our married period.

To avoid some of the problems created by shifting from "just living with" to married, look for areas where a child's feelings can get snagged:

• Has he (she) been excluded from the wedding plans? Have the upcoming plans taken away attention from the children? Is there a lot of commotion in the house, maybe lots of gifts, with nobody doing anything special for the children? Feeling left out is a terrible feeling that sometimes even frightens the groom. Think about the kids.

• Will the child's life change because of the marriage? Will the crowded little apartment that Mr. and Mrs. Right shared as roommates be traded in for a spacious house now that everything is legal? Will the kids be going to a new house—strange bedroom and new surroundings? Does the move include a new school and giving up the neighborhood gang? Making new friends? (Ugh!) Does the new stepparent expect to be called by a different name now that things are "different"? Is there suddenly some confusion about last names and maybe a feeling of not belonging in the new family? Are new siblings overpowering?

• Is there more to accept than just meets the eye? Indeed, is the child just now realizing that his natural parents will not be remarrying as he had planned? Has the child been blocking out reality?

• Is it all hitting the kids at once? If the child has yet to grieve a dead parent or mourn a divorce, he will not take well to the added confusion of a wedding. He may feel you betrayed the dead parent by remarrying and show his anguish only after the wedding takes place—the wedding symbolizing a new life he is unwilling to accept. Just as adults need time between marriages, so do children.

The Weekend Stepparent

For divorced couples living in the same city, the noncustodial parent usually sees his (her) children on weekends. The most common arrangement is every other weekend, although every weekend or every third weekend are not uncommon variations on the same theme.

Seeing the kids every other weekend doesn't really come out to be a whole lot of time, or so rationalizes the good-natured stepparent who is quick to figure out that four days a month can't possibly be too much to give up of one's life. Anyone can get through four days a month, we tell ourselves, incredulous that it should seem such an unbearable burden. Yet the weekend stepmother has the most difficult of the many custodial arrangements by the very fact of the construction of the pact. She is a noncustodial parent. She has no role, no place in the kid's lives. They usually don't need her and may not want her. She has strangers coming and going in her home as if they owned the place, yet treating her as if she were the hostess. (Somehow children never, ever send thank-you notes.) She is not an authority figure and can be belittled by so much as a phone call across town. Her life is violated, allowed to return to normal, and then violated again—almost like a gang rape. It's the least enviable position a stepparent can be in. Almost any type of step-arrangement is better than being a weekend stepmother. (If you think it's easy and you're having fun, skip this chapter.)

Weekend stepparenting is not solely a weekend proposition. It is a full-time change in your life. Most weekend parents lead two entirely different lives, especially when there are no children in their daily existence. The stress of constantly switching back and forth between two ways of life is aging, and emotion-packed. There's anticipational strain—just knowing that they're coming soon may be enough to ruin your day. There are few people who have children walk in and out of their lives and don't react to the changes wrought. And there are even fewer who don't get angry at having to make these constant adjustments.

How To Prepare For The Weekend

Being well-prepared for the kids' arrival and the ensuing changes in your life will make everything that is about to happen to you a lot easier to handle. You're going to have to take some time out from one of your life-styles to devote to your weekend parental life-style in order to best cope with the lifeline shuttle. Make up a checklist, Xerox it, and run over it step by step before the kids come—days before the kids come—before each visit. Don't expect you have enough stuff left over from the last visit and don't need to prepare for this week. You can never be too prepared and you can be woefully unprepared. Don't do your checking two hours before the kids come or in the car on the way to pick them up. Be so prepared that you can accomplish these tasks while you're doing stuff for yourself, so you won't resent extra time spent on the kids. Space out the tasks if you need to, but be sure you do them a day or two before the kids arrive so you never need to suffer last minute panic and anger.

The Freezer. DO keep the freezer well-stocked, preferably all the time. Buy things that go quickly (yes, milk freezes), and stock up. Keep a few separately wrapped hamburger patties on hand and some pizzas, as well as other quick-and-easy-to-eat family favorites. Have a whole dinner, or at least some spaghetti sauce, put away in case of an emergency.

The Shelves. DO buy two of everything. Not only food staples, but toilet paper and cleaning supplies. And if there are a lot of kids, or if you get a lot of traffic, buy *lots* of certain things: soft drinks by the case, half a dozen bottles of apple juice. If you've got the space in the kitchen, make it work for you. Don't forget to buy the largest size on the market; it's always cheaper and you'll use it up.

Kiddie Favorites. DO stock up on the things the kids like to eat, use, and do—if you approve. Brand loyalty is sometimes important to a child because of advertising or habit. Kids usually like to eat the same things (and this means brands) in both homes, although a lot of manipulation goes on in this area when children insist they must have something they have at home when in fact they don't have that item at home. But it is nice to see your favorite something bought just for you in the refrigerator awaiting your arrival. Try to know the favorite treat of each of the kids and stay well-stocked. But don't have your feelings hurt when the old fave gets replaced, and you feel like a fool for not knowing or anticipating the newest craze or craving.

Laundry. DO make sure you're prepared to handle the increased laundry load. Have clean towels and sheets ready. If each child has his own set, so much the better. While you shouldn't be responsible for their laundry, household items should be laundered ahead of time for your own convenience. Nothing is worse than having to run around with a house full of kids you haven't seen in a few weeks while preparing dinner and doing the laundry at the same time. It's not worth it. Their clean clothes are someone else's problem; clean linens are yours.

Gas. DO fill the gas tank before you pick up the kids. Unless you're planning a trip, a full tank will get you through the weekend and will spare you the inconvenience of having to fill up with a car full of screaming kids. (Of course, if yours don't scream, ignore this thought.)

Clean Up. There are two schools of thought on the clean-up category: (1) Why Clean Up: they're only going to mess it up again; and (2) Make Neat: so they don't tell their mother you're a slob and so you can force them to clean up after themselves when you start fighting over what they've done to your nice clean house.

If the child, or children, have their own room or place in your house, do check to see it's how they like it or left it. If someone else has been sleeping in his bed, check the room to see if it has signs of the former guest or the child. You don't want your kids running around like Momma and Papa Bear complaining that someone has been sleeping in their bed.

Schedule. DO make sure you've got the schedule worked out ahead of time. If you plan on a family picnic, and suddenly find one child has to be at a birthday party and the other has a dancing lesson and you're driving both, you may get a little angry. Check obligations with the natural parents. There must be some communication with the ex-spouse, or you will have lots of trouble in this area. (We had considerable trouble when we would tell Amy that we were going backpacking for the weekend and she would arrive with only dresses and white patent leather shoes. She forgot about the backpacking and her mother packed whatever she felt like packing. Maddening.)

And while you're going over the checklist, occasionally make sure you have these items on hand:

1. Complete medicine chest ready for childhood emergencies. (See page 197.)

2. Camera and film.

3. Emergency phone numbers next to the phone.

4. List of baby-sitters.

5. Rainy day doings. (See Chapter 8.)

6. Extra gifts or rewards for visiting or surprises, or birthday parties you weren't told about.

7. Lunch if you're sending a child to school on Monday.

8. Umbrellas (maybe child size).

9. Coats and sweaters for changes in weather; jeans or dress-up clothes for changes in plans.

What To Provide For The Kids

All you really need to provide for the kids are room, board, and clothing. Everything else is an extra. There are a few provisions, however, that will probably make everyone a good bit happier and will serve to unite your family into a more cohesive one.

Every child should have his own space (physical not mental). This isn't to say you have to sell your home and move to a mansion with five bedrooms so each kid can have his own room. It does mean that you have to realize that kids are people and that even if they share your home for a total of four days a month, to feel like part of your lives they need a space of their own. It doesn't have to be a big space; it certainly doesn't have to be a whole room. But it does have to be private and all his. A closet can be made over successfully as a kid's cubbyhole. It's a small thing, but important.

When Mike and I were first married, we lived in a one-bedroom apartment in Manhattan. We always considered the apartment an incredible find: high ceilings with mouldings, a huge bedroom, a good-sized bathroom with an old-fashioned tub that more than compensated for the lousy kitchen and its half-size refrigerator. The rent was reasonable (for New York City), and we would have hung onto the apartment forever.

Until we became parents. Suddenly our "find" would have been better off lost. We had no place for Amy; Amy had no place for herself. She and I shared a closet and a dresser, she slept on the sofa bed in the living room (which I graciously allowed to be adorned with a collection of Snoopy dolls though I was constantly incredulous that my gorgeous furniture had come to this). In choosing a home, we never thought about a child and in acquiring a child we were unable to move. It was unfair to Amy and to us.

When you have several children, you need to account for housing them as well as any stepsiblings that may come with the new family. How you match up the children, and who you ask to share what can be as difficult as negotiating a Middle East peace. Go slowly and carefully: never underestimate the power of scared children.

You should also provide the child, or children, with an atmosphere conducive to their health, education, and well-being—but not at the expense of your own. The biggest difference between a parent and a baby-sitter is the amount of stimulation in the equation. Almost anyone can plunk the kids in front of a TV set, fix a hamburger, and make sure they don't play with matches. Only a parent or parental substitute can provide for their mental and physical growth. A second home that is conducive to loving and growing is a lot more healthy for a child of two families than one in which the stepmother is taking the side of her own children while complaining about the ex-wife and the child-support payments.

You should also think about providing other kids. Childless parents seldom know about the importance of other children to their child's happiness. Many step-families believe that the kids can play with friends during the week and should have family time on the rare occasions they are with their second family. Children still have the best times with other children (once over the age of two or three, and especially over the age of ten), and life may be made considerably easier for you, and them, if you dig up a few kids and provide an atmosphere conducive to play and friendship.

Setting The House Rules

Households don't function without rules. And rules in a secondary home make the difference between a home and a hotel. A large percent of the mothers interviewed for this book said they were surprised to learn that there were rules in their children's second homes—they always assumed that the child went away for the weekend to some never-never land at daddy's house where there were no rules. It's easy to get this misconception because of the two different life-styles that might be prevailing and because of the guilt involved by a parent who may think his children have had such a tough time since the divorce that they should have it easy on the few weekends spent with dad.

As a stepparent, male or female, you must feel free to have a say in the house rules and the enforcement thereof. If you cannot enforce these rules, you are powerless to your stepchildren and they will know it within minutes. You can quit right then. The house rules should be agreed upon by the adults and equally enforced. A stepparent who is afraid to enforce a house rule deserves the lack of respect he is initiating. And the parents must stick together on the rules and their enforcement.

When I was a child, I thought the cruelest thing in the world was the fact that my parents always backed each other up. "Wait till Daddy gets home," I would warn my mother, certain that Daddy would point out the error of her ways. To my chagrin, Daddy always sided with Mommy.

When the two natural parents agree on the house rules and their enforcement, the task of raising a child in two households is immeasurably lightened. What's right in one house is right again and what's wrong is equally wrong. Unfortunately, particularly in split homes, the values don't always mesh. I maintain that my husband and Nancee would still be married if they had the same values. Their opinions on child raising are as different as Adam and Eve's, as are their ideas on discipline.

To make life easier:

• Set the rules as early as possible. Make them clear and simple, easy to understand. If punishment is to be suffered for ignoring the rules, lay it out now—equally as clear and simple. (Hanging at dawn.)

• If you have a lot of children—and they can read—type out and Xerox copies of the house rules and tack them on bedroom doors, bathroom walls, and refrigerator outsides. Or use slogans on cardboard: Rinse tub after using; did you fill gas tank?; make your bed, etc.

• Have the authority to punish transgressors, but make sure the punishment fits the crime and that no child suffers or benefits because of favoritism.

How To Organize Your Space To Allow For The New Additions

Here's my own list of what a kid must have and would be nice to have, for noncustodial parents. There is a book on the market called *A Child's Place* by Alexandra Stoddard which is about decorating children's rooms.

I recommend that if you have the space for your children, let them have their own or shared rooms. Unfortunately, there is no book that tells you how to double-use your space, converting easily from den to child's room and back again every other weekend.

THE KID MUST HAVE:

• A bed, mattress, sleeping bag, or pallet of his or her own.

• One piece of furniture that's his alone. A cubbyhole will do, but a nightstand or a small chest would be preferable. This is a private territory for the child alone and is hands-off-to-parents-and-siblings. It should have a few personal items that stay in your home year-round.

• A drawer of his own, his own hangers and pegs (preferably adjusted to his height), and a space in the bathroom for toothbrush and medicines. Stepchildren who live out of suitcases feel like stepchildren. (Even Cinderella had a place of her own.)

• A place at the dining table that isn't makeshift.

(Our dining table at one time only fit two people so Amy ate on a corner in a very awkward position until we got a new table.)

• A place in the car. There are lots of cars that only seat two. A kid will get a bit fed up pretty soon—so will you—if there's no place for him in the car.

IT WOULD BE NICE TO HAVE:

• A children's room—either a separate bedroom or playroom for several kids in which each child has his own space. The room should be decorated for (and with) the children and should meet their needs. Use color to divide the room into different "private" areas, or for different functions. Consider bunk beds or a stack of fabric-covered mattresses or mats if you have a lot of kids. Don't put too many kids in one room and expect success. Each child should have at least ten-by-ten feet of space to himself.

• A play area where it's okay for kids to be kids. A backyard that is child proofed and safe, or a playroom for games and playmates. Everything should be easily cleaned and include a table for arts and crafts projects and homework, a supply of crayons, magic markers, paper, and paste. Blocks for younger children. Adequate light for all these activities. Your play space needn't be designed by an interior decorator or furnished lavishly—Salvation Army surplus will do, just so it's safe and easily cleaned. Small-sized "children's" furniture is usually outgrown before the payments end and not worth the price. You can make the playroom a family project and have everyone help out with painting and organizing.

• Another line on your phone is something to consider if your children are over ten, and you can't stand never being able to use your phone. The phone company has several special services which don't cost as much as a separate line but provide additional access lines for about four dollars a month. It could very well be worth it to you.

● A closet for the kid's stuff—his winter jackets you keep on hand even in the summer, his sleeping bags, games no longer used, etc. Or just a kid's private space built into a closet—no adults allowed, pets okay.

● Equal space for part-time children who must bunk in with full-time children. If you expect the full-time children to share all their things graciously, you're dumb.

TIPS FOR COMBINING PART-TIME CHILDREN IN ONE PART-TIME ALL-PURPOSE ROOM:

● If you are combining a guest room and a child's room, make sure to personalize the room in the child's favor. Something so grown up or fancy he feels like a guest is alienating. If the room is very "decorated," make sure there are teddy bears or whatever on the bed, and places for the child's collections and favorite things. His own set of sheets and towels would be a nice touch. If you are using a sofa bed instead of a regular bed, make sure it's the kind a child can use easily himself. Avoid formality in this room if at all possible.

● Make use of the pillow furniture craze and use a lot of cube-shaped sofas, chairs, and ottomans that can be built into different modular arrangements, providing a sofa and two chairs and then rearranging into sleeping space for several. You can buy large foam cubes, cover them with sheet fabric, or any inexpensive material, and stack them. Or you can have mattresses upholstered and stack them for use as a sofa (three make a great sofa) and then let the kids sleep on the individual parts.

● Give your child a permanent space of his own by subdividing your extra room. A loft makes a great space for a kid, as does a partitioned cubicle.

The One-Month Or Summer Stepparent

You may have never thought about it before, but it is enormously easier to be a one-month or summer stepparent than any other kind. And if the divorced parties live in separate cities, it's even easier.

Time is on the side of the one-month stepparent. There is enough time to establish your own identity, to create a relationship, to see things through. Noncustodial parents get to feel like real parents; stepchildren get to see you as a real person rather than a weekend figure. Besides, once you've got the kids figured out, why not capitalize on your progress? Keep them for a month—or the summer—and say good-bye till Christmas.

I began my instant motherhood as a One-Month-in-the-Summer Mother. I found the first three days devastating and the first three weeks crippling. I can't even report on the fourth week because I was semiconscious most of the time. But I had a great time. My inability to cope was all a matter of unpreparedness on my part and a case of trying to do too much. I learned for the next summer and certainly had it better than any weekend stepmother when you consider these facts:

● Statistics show that stepchildren and stepparents living in the same family unit and functioning as one family have the greatest ratio of happiness in a step-situation.

● There isn't an extra parent to get in the way. You're the mommy, he's the daddy, and you both fall into more traditional roles.

● When you wake up the next day, they'll still be there. It's a bit hard to establish rules and form any lasting bonds with anyone who arrives on Saturday and departs on Sunday.

• The two worldedness of two-family children is easier to cope with when completely separated. Kids can "start over" every year as they shuttle between separate homes and life-styles. Amy specifically asked us not to move to California because she liked to come to New York for a month and be treated like a princess. (Who wouldn't?)

• You can build something. There's even time to fight and work out a solution.

If you do live in the same city as the ex-spouse, your separate lives won't have as much of a quality of adventure to them and the children may not adapt as quickly. Sometimes it's hard to live two different lives in a community where you're used to one style of living.

How To Prepare For The Kids' Arrival

Summer or one-month parents spend a large percentage of their time either without children at all or in one life-style, and only a short period of time in their other life-style.

For people without children, the switch is naturally more dramatic. But for the mother of one toddler, who suddenly finds her house filled with teenagers, the shift can be dramatic—and traumatic.

Somehow or another, it always gets to be that time of the year again when the kids arrive. Being prepared for the event, way before it happens, will make it all easier. Although you may be vaguely aware that they are coming soon enough, may even have made some nebulous plans that you've told yourself have settled the issue ("How 'bout if we get a camper and drive to Mexico?"), the time to switch into Active Parent is not the day before the kids step off the plane. It's the month before.

Use this checklist to see how prepared you are. Make your own checklist to fit your personal situation and use it every year.

Travel Arrangements: Know who is responsible for the travel arrangements and who pays for what. Special rates are often available by booking in advance. Don't expect his new wife to be doing something she expects him to be doing while he is expecting you to do it. Make sure that when the reservations are made the kids arrive and depart at times that are convenient for you. You don't want to have to take off a day of work to go meet the kids. Confirm all travel details the night or day before the trip is being made for any last minute changes you may have been left out of.

Space: Make sure your kids' space is ready and well-appointed. Does it meet the needs of children who have grown a year since you saw them last? If new linens, draperies, or mattresses are required, know about it in advance. Be able to plan for the expense of these purchases rather than suffer the shock of needing new everything.

Plans: Have your time together planned ahead of time. You're taking a house at the beach and the kids will play outdoors all day. They're going to camp. You're all going camping. Tennis lessons in the mornings, swimming in the afternoon. If you don't have plans, drop everything and make some. Remember that summer is a busy season and you may have to book early to get what you want. There are many camps, particularly day camps, with one-week sessions that will meet your needs. Book in advance.

Children: While you're making plans, make sure there's someone to enjoy them with. If you live on a block or in a building with a lot of children, you may have your needs taken care of. Kids need other kids to play with. Go out and find some immediately. It's probably more important they be the same sex than the same age.

Help: If your life-style will change radically when the kids arrive, you may need some help in coping with it all. Make sure your baby-sitter list is up to date and active for summer. If you are considering live-in help, a nanny or a mother's helper, be sure to book in advance. You just may find it worthwhile to save for eleven months to get some help for the twelfth month when the house is filled with children.

Save: You know that the kids are coming, but are you saving for their arrival? We expect to get wiped out in December as we buy Christmas gifts. Have you anticipated the cost of the children's summer stay with you and are you prepared? Amy always ended up costing us one thousand extra dollars no matter how I arranged or rearranged the summer. We didn't always happen to have an extra thousand dollars under the mattress and had to start saving for her visits a few months before she came. Granted, we always planned humdinger visits with lots of travel and excitement, but I never found a camp that was less expensive. Just doing nothing also costs money.

How To Make It Through
The Last Week

No matter how long Amy was staying with us, it always seemed a bit too long. Not much too long, just a bit too long. Maybe a week—or five days. Everything would be going along perfectly and we were the happiest family in the world, then without any reason, everything would go wrong and I would suddenly begin to resume my murder plans. I found myself taking Valium at an increased rate, grinding my teeth in my sleep, and blaming everything on premenstrual distress, whether it was appropriate or not. Our marriage suddenly was not worth it; the wonderful child I adored sprouted a tail and horns. Why hadn't we planned to send her home earlier? Could we send her home today? Would I survive?

After two years of this syndrome (in which we did not keep her the same amount of time), I suddenly realized that we were plagued by Last Week Frustration, a more or less normal thing to happen to groups of people in a time warp of ending one life-style and beginning another. We had already had whatever wild adventures we were going to have, we had already discovered all of each other's new secrets, and read all the Pippi Longstocking we could stand. And we were all anticipating the next change—back to mommy or back to childless. We were all so uncomfortable with each other it was boring. Amy knew she was leaving, we knew she was leaving, and we were still stuck together a few more days.

This phenomenon, by the way, is somewhat akin to the Sunday Evening Squabble Syndrome in which everyone fights because of the weekend shift from one household to the other.

But there is a real easy way to beat the problem: save the best for last and make sure it's exhausting. The grand finale, I've decided, isn't at the end by accident. While we are always delighted to see the kids and shower them with gifts, attention, and a let's-do-everything-immediately attitude, it works much better to start out slowly and work up to a bang. Whatever the one special treat you have planned for the kids, make sure it covers the last week. And then say good-bye.

When To Send Them Home Early

Despite your fine plans, it may not work out. Sometimes you just can't stand it anymore. Sometimes you think you'll die if you have to do their wash one more day ... or hear their voices or listen to what they call music or feed their stupid friends, etc. Sometimes it pays to send them home early and avoid a final, frustrating week that can shatter all the good things you've built up during the stay.

Sending them home early is one of the most unfortunate parts of being a stepparent because it's so unrelated to the real world. If these were your kids, you would have no place to send them home to, so you'd just muddle through whatever the problem is and come out stronger. But then again, you wouldn't be forced into planning grand finales and special entertainment for children you see every day of your life.

There's a terribly fine line between sending them home for the right reasons and sending them home for the wrong reasons, and you need to give it real thought rather than emotion. Likewise with threatening to send the child home. I had a great tactic whereby whenever Amy didn't do what she was supposed to—and if sufficiently angered—I threatened to put her on the next plane. It's doubtful I really would have. (No matter how much I wanted to send her back, I invariably forgave her.) I am sure I made the threats because my father had used similar tactics on me and it was a nasty trick I knew well. When visitation is the one thing the parents hold over each other, it's childish and maybe harmful to put the child in a position of having to behave to stay in someone's home. The child is yours, for better or for worse, and if you don't get through the low points together, there won't be any high points.

On the other hand, everyone involved in a second family has to lessen the stigma of leaving early. We become so afraid of hurting each other's feelings that we may be reluctant to admit we've had enough—when perhaps the kids have had it too, and everyone would be happier quitting early. Young children can't stand to be away from their mothers for a long time and as heroic as they try to be, they often get homesick. You cannot take it personally when a child wants to go home early. You should not make that child feel guilty about his needs.

There must be a difference between sending the kids home early in anger and sending them home early in mutual agreement and love . . . or even semimutual agreement. (You may not want to let them go, but find that it's the best thing to do.) Obviously, there are no set rules on how to decide when it's time to go home, but look for these signs:

• Last Week Frustration or Sunday Night Syndrome.

• The Blahs. No matter what you do or what you promise or how much the kids usually like it, no one cares now.

• Stepped up fighting with siblings, stepsiblings, and peers.

• Crying, headaches, or attention-getting devices including feigned illness.

• Talk only of the future, while most kids can hardly wait till Monday, etc. When the child can only talk about going home, his mommy (daddy), and familiar regulars of his other life, maybe it's time to go.

We once had a situation with Amy in which everything was going beautifully. Each day I congratulated myself on my genius at finally having mastered the art of summer mothering. (This was my third try.) We had one more week together and I was looking forward to it because I had carefully orchestrated the grand finale. Amy, it seems, was confused as to when it was she was supposed to be going home. I was quite clear on when she was going home, as it was marked in my calendar and had been confirmed with Nancee. I did not take into account, however, the fact that we had taken Amy two days early in order to go camping. She knew she was staying a month, which in her mind was thirty days. She counted off thirty and decided it must mean she was leaving on day thirty, despite the plans. At least, that's what I am assuming happened. No one knows for sure. Anyway, in a casual phone conversation, Nancee said she'd be over on Wednesday to pick Amy up. Wednesday? That wasn't right; Amy wasn't supposed to go home until Sunday. Wednesday would be smack dab in the middle of my grand finale.

I hit the ceiling as anger flowed like hot lava, steaming and gurgling. If Amy wanted to go home early, all she had to do was say something. She had been given plenty of opportunities to leave because we knew she gets homesick. How she could not even have told us that she had made plans to leave early was beyond us. The thought that Nancee could have just arrived and Amy would have walked out the door while we would have had our mouths open in amazement was too much to bear. Struck dumb with anger, my husband and I packed Amy's things and immediately drove her home, telling her how disappointed we both were. Disappointed is an adult word. I was shattered. I felt rejected, used, unappreciated, and furious. How dare she let me pay for the grand finale, plan it for a month, talk about it almost daily, and then blithely walk out without so much as an explanation?

Neither Mike nor I did the adult thing by packing Amy off. We were both furious and acted emotionally. I'm sure we were also reacting to three summers of catering to her every whim and three summers of confusion at misunderstanding our role in her life. We all would have grown a bit had we kept her and worked it out.

Had the same thing happened in New York, we probably would have gone to bed and forgotten it in the morning.

The real problem was one of rejection, and I think we needed to know we were in control of the situation, that we held the ultimate weapon. We could live without her. If she wasn't willing to conform to our rules, we would show her the door. We had to know that there was a line; that there were some things that we would not tolerate. We had to prove that we were the bosses and that she could not control our lives; that her demand was not our pleasure; that everything she did was not always hunky-dory. Until the night we took her home early, we had changed our lives for her—made her the center of our world. We needed to know that we were the center of our own world, that our marriage was more important than her manipulations. It is unfortunate that we couldn't work out the problem with a joke, a talk, and a better understanding of what probably was a simple misunderstanding.

But kicking Amy out was a new beginning for Mike and me. We've had a lot of tears and anger since the night she went, but we have gained a better perspective of ourselves and our marriage because of it. I don't recommend getting rid of your kids to test anything or anyone. But it could be a very positive, important part of your relationship. The night we sent Amy home was the night we regained control of our lives and our future together. It was one of the hardest, but wisest things we ever did.

Guilt Of The One-Month Parent

Guilt plays an important part in everyone's child-rearing methods. If you really want to see guilt, suggest to a noncustodial parent that you send his (her) children to camp while they visit you.

As Amy's first visit approached, I asked Mike what he planned to do with her. Clearly he had it all thought out because he answered immediately and with confidence. He explained that on the first weekend we'd go up to our house in the country, on the second we'd go to Boston, on the third we'd go to Washington, and on the fourth we'd be back at the house.

"But what about the days in between?" I asked, desperate for a rational answer. He had quite forgotten about the days in between, thinking they would go as quickly for Amy as they did for us. "I'll take her to the office with me," he answered smugly.

That didn't sound great to me so I suggested she go to day camp. I thought that was a brilliant suggestion for someone who hadn't seen or heard about day camp in over twenty years. I congratulated myself until Mike raged and screamed at me in a manner making me believe that he didn't like my brilliant idea. He shouted that he hadn't seen her in a year, that he wasn't flying her three thousand miles to go to day camp, that she was his daughter, and they needed to reaffirm their dedication to each other. No camp, do you hear me, no camp. And that was that.

Although I never did understand why I couldn't convince him of my plan's merit, I did understand guilt. The noncustodial parent suffers an incredible amount of guilt at not being part of his child's daily growth. The guilt of the out-of-town, noncustodial parent is even stronger.

The guilt, I've found, sometimes spreads. In a year or two I too had symptoms of the same epidemic—I felt guilty by association with a noncustodial parent. I found myself feeling guilty if I didn't provide my stepdaughter with all the things she didn't get at home. The social worker inside me rejected normalcy and took on projects contrived to ease the guilt I felt in not contributing to Amy's growth all year round. We both went nuts when it came to guilt, which is a common problem in part-time parents.

In fact, few parents have been able to leave home and children without feeling guilt every now and then. The problem is how much and how to control it. Obviously if your guilty feelings are invading your ability to cope rationally, it's time for a little professional help. If your guilt is occasional and lasts for a small amount of time, it's normal and needs to be accepted as such. If guilt is making you and your mate arrive at unnecessary decisions, it's time to back off and reexamine the situation. In the light of how difficult it was to take Amy to work with us, day camp should have been the perfect solution. Learn the parameters of what you can handle and stick to them. You can't do what you can't do and therefore shouldn't feel guilty about it.

The Holiday Stepparent

Almost all stepparents get the children for holidays or portions of holidays. Whether you are a summer parent or a weekly parent, you will still do your share of holiday parenting as well. Holidays are so important to parents that child custody on specific holidays is usually written into the divorce settlement and is legally enforceable.

If you have no children of your own, you probably have a very special definition of a holiday: long weekends off in the country as lovers; trips to secluded Caribbean islands; free time to clean the oven and paint the kitchen. Maybe a trip to some wild and wonderful world hideaway that took a year's savings.

You'll find that these holidays cease to exist when you become a stepparent. After all, holidays were really created to free children from the bondage of school and are therefore owed to the kids as their own special reward for existing. Or so they think. Children believe that holidays were made for them and that every parent's obligation is to see that the kids have a good time and are properly entertained while on holiday.

So when you share a child, you share holidays. You can handle these holidays however you please. In our family we've tried them together (awful) and separately (two Christmases). We've also had to cope with religious differences because Mike's former wife is not the same religion we are and is not raising Amy in any religion.

While Mike and I have often thought of escaping to the south of France, or taking a few days off to maybe go to the Napa Valley, our vacations are now confined to school holidays. When Easter break falls is of utmost importance to our plans, ditto the last day of school, which has no regard for Memorial Day, and Labor Day weekend. We can never just get up and go. First we have to ascertain whose turn it is for the approaching holiday. Then we have to ascertain that we are indeed using the established schedule, as it's possible that Nancee had planned to switch a holiday with us but hadn't mentioned it yet. Then we have to plan our plans. Meanwhile, every other family in America has gone through the same rigmarole and we are all traveling at peak times. Months ahead of time we are forced to make reservations we don't know if we'll be keeping. Yet we also cannot stay home and plan nothing because we know Amy will be bored enough to make us miserable.

The simplest solution is to accept, right from the beginning, that when you marry a person with a child, your holidays will change. Your life changed, so why shouldn't your holidays? You should prepare for each holiday visit the way you prepare for each summer or month-long visit. If the holiday stay is to be longer than a weekend, use the summer planning guide and checklist (page 115). A week-long vacation can seem like a month if you're not pre-pared—especially on holidays where some places of busi-ness may be closed, others too crowded, and weather conditions unfavorable.

Know what you're going to do with the kids before they arrive. Have back up plans in case of a snowstorm, or whatever local disaster could change your plans. Know who is picking up the kids, how they are getting to your house, who is paying for their travel, when they are to be returned, and if they are missing school.

Expect these changes in your daily routine:

• Children get up early in the morning. If you planned on sleeping late, toss a coin with your mate and al-ternate as to who gets up to take care of the kids. Teach them how to make breakfast for themselves. Tell them you are not to be disturbed if you think you can get away with it.

• Children make noise. If you are planning to sleep late, are you well-armed? Earplugs? Blinders? Sleep machine? Or will you be furious when their childish noises (bang-bang, you're dead!—I am not!) penetrate your inner sanctum? Even after you are awake, are you ready for the new noise level you are about to live with?

• Children eat. Okay, everyone eats. But your chil-dren might not eat what adults eat. Or they might need to be fed at an earlier hour. Or you may find yourself looking for a new set of restaurants that tolerate children's peculiar eating habits. You may always eat Christmas dinner at mid-night but find that your kids can't wait that long.

• Children get bored. Because many holidays are long weekends in which you are looking forward to peace-ful relaxation, you forget that the children don't want the same. They're full of energy, and you want to lounge by the pool and read or sit by the fire of the ski lodge and do the crossword puzzle. Bored children make for cranky children and cranky children can make everyone miserable. When you travel on a holiday, make sure you know what facilities will be available to the children. Checking ahead of time may avert disaster. Plan holiday activities that use up energy. I always figure that if I can exhaust the children I'm with—preferably without killing myself—I've won a major battle.

• Children have to be back at school. In our holiday travels I have always found myself rushing around making desperate reservations that fit within the scope of the school holiday. Needless to say, every other parent is doing the same thing, and travel schedules become bogged down with the good flights already filled. Traffic is worse than usual; Amy complains about the crowds at airports because she says she always gets bonked on the head with a handbag; the luggage is more apt to get lost. It's a drag. So I keep Amy out of school a day longer and life becomes much simpler. We leave the day after everybody else and return the day after everybody else. Nancee has never complained about the day of school Amy misses, so we have no difficulties with her. Everyone has a better time.

How To Keep The Kids From Ruining Your Holiday

With so many changes occurring when children join your holidays, it's easy to hate them and feel cheated. You're more apt to let a holiday get ruined because you're anxious to blame anything on the kids. But it doesn't have to work that way. You can have a great time on holidays with children—if you are willing to let yourself.

Define your idea of a happy holiday. Both mates should do this. There may be a huge discrepancy right there—even before the kids arrive—that could lead to further holiday troubles. What are the kind of places and things you would ideally like to do? What would it take to make Christmas terrific for you? Weed out the extraneous elements and stick to a basic list of what you need for your holiday to be a happy one. Make sure you get what you want, or what is reasonable to get. If you get some of the things on your list and know they were obtained just to make you happy, you should feel a lot better. (If you don't feel better, you're a sore sport.)

Label problem areas ahead of time. What do you hate about the holidays? See if together you can make sure to avoid the things you dislike. Even if it's having the children, maybe you can be less involved with them and have a better holiday.

Make the plans revolve around you. A holiday is a time when someone can easily feel left out—especially by a precreated family. If you are the star of the family and everything includes you, you may feel a lot better about the occasion. Things change when you're involved. Don't go off in the corner and sulk—get involved in some activities and make them revolve around you.

Don't get blue thinking your life is ruined forever. Children grow and change and your holidays will too. One of the biggest mistakes stepparents make is assuming that things will always be as bad as they are now.

Set your expectations at a low level. You know what mother said about it being better to give than to receive. Get your holiday joy from giving and don't worry about receiving. Don't even think about it. I once made myself miserable for three weeks before Mother's Day hating Amy for not including me. As it was, Amy showed up for Mother's Day with a beautifully wrapped box containing the world's most gorgeous (and expensive) nightgown, hand picked by Amy, and paid for by her mother. Had I expected nothing, I would have been terribly surprised and pleased. As it was, I was surprised and pleased, but only after several weeks of self-inflicted frustration.

Picking the right present for a new parent is very difficult, so even if you get presents on gift-giving occasions, you can't expect them to be perfect at first. Appreciate anything you get and consider yourself lucky to be remembered.

Plan a thank-God-it's-over gift or party for yourself. Just make sure you get it right away. If it's a day off all alone, a little something you've wanted but didn't care to splurge on, whatever; you deserve it.

Religious Differences And How To Handle Them

One of the things that may change drastically in the stepparents' holiday season is the way in which the holidays are celebrated when there are a variety of traditional and religious experiences to choose from. Usually, everyone wants a holiday to be like it was in his childhood. With a combined family you have a lot of memories, and maybe a few religions that might not appear to mix. You have two choices: (1) Celebrate the holiday your own way in private, or (2) Combine it all together and create your own new religion and traditions.

Without trying to convert anyone, you can celebrate a wide range of religious festivities that will enhance the holiday and make it unique to your family. Add your childhood memories to theirs, and then maybe throw in a few new thoughts—you can involve the children in researching how the holidays were celebrated in different countries, times, and by different religions. If the religious parts of holidays need explaining, make it interesting to children.

Be prepared to give up some of your family traditions in order to make room for new ones. I came from a family that did not celebrate Christmas and I had to do a lot of thinking before deciding if I wanted Christmas to be celebrated in my new family. I finally decided it was fine, as long as we also celebrated Hanukkah.

If you are unable to settle the religious differences in your family through combined efforts or private observance, it's time for a family meeting and perhaps guidance from your clergyman.

Holiday Grandparents

Holidays are synonymous with family times, and you may soon find yourself combining your instant family with your traditional family. My parents were not thrilled that I married a man with a child and did not take immediately to the idea of being grandparents. Just as I became an instant mother, they became instant grandparents—with no preparation or time to get used to the idea. In fact, we didn't even ask if they wanted to be grandparents. We told them they were grandparents, because we wanted Amy to have another set of grandparents. We initiated the decision with a Christmas visit. My mother was named Grandma Glo since Amy already had a Grandma Flo. (I thought that was cute.)

Grandma Glo felt she was too young to become a grandmother, particularly a grandmother of an eight-year-old child, but she bravely (and silently, I might add) accepted her new rank. My father thought Amy was adorable and took to her immediately. My sister said Aunt Debbie was too much for her and Debra would be fine; my brother was everything an Uncle Steve should be and became Amy's new best friend. By the second day of our visit, Amy had successfully joined my family and was actively helping bring in the New Year as my family had done for decades.

Mother had done her homework and was prepared with a list of baby-sitters, neighborhood children, and G-rated movies. She had called the pony stables, tennis clubs, and zoos for their schedules and rates and had them listed by the phone. I found a Dr. Spock and a Gesell at her bedside, along with the phone number of the pediatrician.

We were very lucky that everything worked out so well and my parents have since become real grandparents to Amy. It's not always as easy, and becomes a lot more involved when there are natural grandchildren as well as step-grandchildren. Many a step-grandparent has felt put in an awkward position by being told to treat a stepchild the same as a grandchild. Usually, the way stepchildren are accepted into a new family depends on:

• Your parents' opinion of your husband and your marriage. Positive feelings bring acceptance and a willingness to try.

• The kids' feelings about taking on another set of grandparents. If the kids don't want the stepparent, they probably don't want step-grandparents.

• Advance planning. You need enough room, food, and time for all members of the family to make the visit work. Use the checklist for summer parents to make sure you, or your parents, are ready for the change in their lives.

• Your own relationship with your parents matters when you bring someone new into your family. If the situation is fragile, do you need the pressure of a step-relationship?

• Timing. If the family combination doesn't work this year, it doesn't mean it will never work. Being an instant grandparent takes time—just like being a stepparent. You can't expect everyone to walk into a comfortable relationship. Hopefully one will build over the years.

The Holiday Exchange Program

Most child custody agreements spell out what holidays which parent gets whom and on what schedule. You may have the every-other rotation or the either-or rotation (You set either Christmas or Hanukkah, but not both).

I entered parenthood thinking it was tacky for a child to celebrate two versions of the same holiday. I thought two Christmases and two birthdays were appalling and that a spirit of competition was created between the parents. I refused to play the game. After we moved to California, we took Amy's presents over to her house for discovery under her own tree on Christmas morning—we could live without being there ourselves. Or so I thought. Then Nancee invited us to be there Christmas morning for a family holiday. Mike and I were charmed. How perfect. We went out and got presents for everyone else who would be there—all Nancee's relatives—and placed them under the tree. We got there, Amy unwrapped scads of gifts cooing that each one was the best in the world. We got nothing. We spent all our savings, and there was nothing for us. We were wrong to expect something, true, but we were green then.

From then on we maintained strictly separate holidays and dual celebrations with either-or options.

We discovered the two-holiday system. It goes like this. We have our Thanksgiving or celebrate with friends and Amy comes over for Thanksgiving. The Thanksgiving she comes for just doesn't happen to be on Thanksgiving

Day. We celebrate her birthday the week after or the week before.

There is usually a tremendous amount of ego involved in holiday celebration, which actually gets in the way of both the real meaning of the holiday and the celebration. If you can separate your feelings of guilt or need to impress the children with your love and devotion, you may be better able to deal with an alternate holiday schedule. If you are using holidays—particularly gift-giving ones—to buy affection or compete with your ex-spouse (Nancee once admitted that she now felt competitive about vacation spots and would always feel she had to take Amy someplace better than we had taken her), you just may come up with a happier family and easier step-relationships if you decide on an alternate method for celebrating holidays.

5.
The Working Stepparent

Life as a Working Stepmother

When I was just a working woman, I had a system. I flew out of bed at 7:15 in the morning, ran quickly through the shower, and jumped into the clothes I had already laid out the night before. I smeared on a little Alexandra de Markoff makeup (because I knew I was worth it), kissed my husband good-bye, and charged out the door, remembering only to toss the morning newspaper on the table as I dashed for the elevator.

I scrambled down the block to the bus, which at this hour of the morning was always empty, and set to work organizing my schedule as best I could between Seventy-ninth and Fifty-second streets. I got juice and a doughnut downstairs and was easily at my desk at 8:15. This was a great system because no one else got into the office until 9:30 and I was able to maintain my demeanor of efficiency without anyone knowing I had to work at it.

Then Amy arrived.

I couldn't fly out of bed at 7:15 because she and I had been playing fairy princess in the middle of the bed since 6:30 A.M. I couldn't jump into the clothes I had laid out because they had been oohed and ahhed and petted and touched with sticky hands so often that they were now useless. I couldn't smear on a little makeup because I didn't have time, nor could I dash out the door and leave the child there because of my archaic belief that families all eat together.

It took no time at all to discover that I had walked into a terrible conflict in life-styles. How could I be the mother my mother was and the working woman I had been for eight years?

I decided to take Amy to work with me. My husband had said he would take her, he promised me he would, but in the light of a new day I am consumed with compassion. I can handle her so much better than he can. (Taking care of children is women's work.) There is a great deal of the martyr in a stepmother and I agreed to take over.

We board the bus. Amy is big for her age. "Hey lady," screams the driver, "that'll be another fifty cents for your kid." "She's under six," I lie. I refuse to pay for Amy. Amy refuses to sit down because she is asking each passenger if she can put his money in the little box. Mothers around me are giving me knowing glances. I stare right in their eyes. I defy them to make me control that kid.

We get to the office. I get two doughnuts and two orange juices, wondering if the child will suffer brain damage from not eating bacon and eggs for breakfast. Will God punish me for not being a good mommy and not making Wheatena?

In the fashion office, we are greeted by the fashion coordinator. His name is Damien York (or so he claims), he is very, very tall and so skinny that you can see each bone individually and every detail of his Adam's apple which roves around his neck when he shrieks, as he is wont to do. He wears wire-rimmed spectacles and has his flopsy-mopsy hair combed evenly across his brow so the layers of henna form a monochromatic halo. He dresses in tight-fitting black and speaks with a slightly phony British accent. "What is that turd doing here?" he asks, pointing a glazed fingernail at Amy.

Now what would you do when someone calls your child—even your stepchild—a turd? ' was ready to murder him.

Damien finally acquiesces and agrees to let Amy play with the clothes while I do my work. As I head for my office I see her race between racks of garments with an umbrella in her hand as she duels with a four hundred and fifty dollar Dimitri suit.

For lunch we have a treat. I invite my friend Ellen to join us at a chic ice cream parlor not far from the office. (Amy can only make it four blocks without getting a headache.) Ellen and I are old business friends who meet almost every week for lunch and discuss executive jobs open to women, how to get as much money as a man for equal work, and what to wear to a sales convention so you look attractive but are taken seriously.

Ellen: Wait till you hear about this new merchandising program I'm initiating. The guys in research and development came up with these incredible statistics that proved that each of our customers was really capable of . . .

Amy: Do you want to see what's in my purse?

Ellen: Not now, sweetheart. Mommy and I are talking business. Anyway, we thought that if we could devise a consumer program whereby . . .

Amy: Mommy, do you have any aspirin? I have a headache. My tummy hurts too. I think I have a fever.

Obviously Amy doesn't apppreciate the fine points of Ellen's merchandising program and Ellen doesn't feel like spending her whole lunch hour talking baby talk. Not that Amy isn't capable of intelligent conversation—it just has to be about her. I have made a dismal boo-boo. A child and an adult cannot mix on any cogent level. I hate Ellen for not taking time out to find something of interest to discuss with Amy. I hate Amy for not being interested in business. I hate myself for being so stupid as to think it would work.

We return to the office where Amy will take her place as my secretary . . . using my typewriter and making a hell of a racket, but having a great time. I suggest she use the office WATS line and call all her friends in California, but the calls have to be put through the office operator and somehow I know she'll recognize Amy's voice. There is only one thing to do: escape the office. As the others stare at me rudely—after all, most of them have children, and they don't bring them to work—I shuffle Amy out the door and off to a movie. At three o'clock on a summer afternoon, in the middle of Manhattan, I can't think of anything else to do with her. We see *The Sound Of Music* for the seventh time. (Amy has since seen it twelve times.) Then we go to the grocery store and stumble home. Amy has had a great day. I am considering suicide.

The Working Stepparent

Being a working stepparent differs from being a plain old working parent in that you may not have the kids all the time and are therefore forced to juggle between continuous shocks: this week you are plain old working people with a weekend to pull yourselves together; next week you're plain old working people with the sudden realization that Wednesday you do shopping for five rather than two. If you work and have children full time, you come to deal with the situation as best you can and make it work for you. If you are only a part-time parent you tend to slough it all off saying, "I can handle this," and thus burdening yourself with a load you would never bend to in real life. We forget that our stepchildren are part of real life; that a working stepparent must make the same allowances a working custodial parent makes.

Both stepfathers and stepmothers have adjustments to make when they work full time and children enter their lives. Leisure time is spent differently; obligations at home are compounded; life is no longer your own. The stepfather must realize that when he comes home at night he will be confronted with the noise of children, as well as the needs of the children. Stepmothers will come home to traditional mother work: fixing dinner and cleaning the kitchen—but tonight she makes her stepson's favorite meal instead of her own and cleans up a few extra places at the table. She too must deal with noise and needs that she may have little interest in providing for.

The biggest mistake working stepparents make is not providing themselves with the additional help any custodial parent wouldn't consider living without. Stepparents need to realize that they are combining two of the world's most difficult situations into one, and that it has to be the hardest job on earth.

Juggling Job And Children

Fathers (even stepfathers) are supposed to work. Society guarantees dad the right to a hard day at the office and the privilege to come home exhausted and slide behind the newspaper with a drink, shutting out the noise of the scrambling kids as he presides over the sofa and the dinner table. Dad's family responsibilities are financial and titular and, even if he isn't the main provider for the children, he is still the main provider for the wife. He isn't expected to worry about how he's going to make everyone's lunch and still get to work on time, or how he will leave work early for the school play when he really has a business meeting scheduled at the same time. Daddies are expected to go to their business meetings; mommies are expected to rearrange their business meetings.

Thus, the art of juggling home duties and office responsibilities has fallen mostly to women. Only liberated men who are able to help with the responsibilities of raising a family are now allowing themselves to share duties that twenty years ago automatically fell into a woman's domain. But the answer to artful juggling lies not in bionic motherhood, superhuman strength, or getting up three hours earlier each morning, but in successfully combining your job and his kids (or vice versa) by redefining the work load. In the New American Family, the husband is going to have to be willing to share the mechanics of family life if he expects that family to function well. The secret to working and wifing lies in the delegation of duties.

From personal experience, I can tell you that there's not much reason for you to try to combine traditional motherhood with a full-time job, unless you are a masochist. Or a scientist. (Or Wonder Woman.) As a scientific study, it might be important for you to know how miserable you can get before you are ready for some realistic changes. Otherwise, accept my word for it. If you have a full and active life as a working woman—whether you are a stewardess or president of a company—your life will have to change somewhat to accommodate a family. Look for those changes up front, so you can regroup and reorganize before you need a month in a quiet corner of a padded cell.

List all your duties. Include a typical day's work and the added duties of a typical day with children. Use two different color pens so you can see the extra tasks you are taking on. Now do you see the difference?

Eliminate the unnecessary. Throw them out. You can't do everything. Accept it now and establish your priorities. Scratch through the unimportant and the postponable.

Discover the buy-outs. Of the tasks on the list, both mother work and office work, which ones can someone else do? Delegate responsibility. What can you pay someone else to do in your home that will free you to do more of what you want to do? What can the kids do? What can your husband do? What *must* you alone do? What do you alone *want* to do?

Reschedule. Have you got rid of enough things? Probably not. Did you leave yourself some free time in every day? Have you programmed late time? Emergencies happen. Give yourself some contingency hours. You may think that you're onto this trick and that you're very clever to have come up with this new list. You're getting warm, but don't be cocky. Eliminate two more things. You're supposed to feel like you're ahead of the game, not coming out even.

Assignments. Everyone should have regular jobs in the running of your household. If they're permanent, or quasi permanent, there's no confusion as to who is doing what. The extra burdens of parenthood should especially be divided up between the stepparent and the natural parent. Grocery shopping for two might be a quick and easy enough chore that a working woman mindlessly accomplishes on her drive home from the office. She can always run into the store and quickly get the makings of dinner for two in about ten minutes. Or she can decide the two partners will go out for dinner, or will make do on what's left in the house. When the kids are coming, the milk you never drink must be purchased, as well as the extra groceries and heavy shopping that cannot be done in ten minutes. Stocking up for the family is a major chore that should not be shunted on one tired person after a hard day at the office. They're his kids? Let him do the grocery shopping. Find a twenty-four-hour grocery store and shop at your convenience. Or shop together and divide up the list. The extra laundry, cooking, cleaning, and driving should be divided equally among the adults and children who are able to help out. The children are not guests in your home and should have duties that are theirs. In our family, Amy is in charge of feeding the cats and changing the kitty litter—a task that is mine during the week. I appreciate her helping out and am pleased that she never forgets to take care of the cats because I take her as a responsible child on the evidence of her faithfulness to this task. While she does not even feed her fish at home, she is faithful to our cats. Children will do different jobs in different homes—what's boring in one household may be a novelty on weekends, when it's not permanent. Insist on the children helping you out.

If you have a big family, have a family bulletin board or duty chart that clearly outlines each person's responsibility. If you are changing styles of operating, hold a family powwow to discuss what's going on. Arbitrary changes (or ones that appear arbitrary) might be confusing to children who are already confused enough. Sit down and talk it out with them; explain that you need help. Few people don't respond to an honest plea for help.

Enjoy. The new arrangement should leave you time for work, time for family duties, time to be together, and time alone. All four should balance—not equally in time, but in harmony with your life-style. If you have no time for the things that are important to you as an individual, you will resent the people who make you take time from yourself. Someone else's children are easy enough to resent, so why ask for trouble? You must unload yourself of family responsibilities to the point of your own happiness. You owe it to yourself. If you contribute to the family welfare, they must contribute to yours.

A Working Schedule

You'll find you juggle best on a schedule. In fact, the only way to combine motherhood and career efficiently is to work on a carefully planned schedule. That's not to say your life has to be so tight that you need to pencil in time to brush your teeth, but you do need to make maximum use of your time.

Know your body type. If you are a morning person, use the mornings to their best advantage and schedule lighter projects in the afternoon. Never do in one time slot what would be better placed in another. Use your personal strength and energy to your own advantage. But remember that you're not a robot. I have two schedules: one for three weeks of the month, another for the week before my period. I used to get frustrated and teary when I couldn't do as much the week before my period. Now I let it work for me and reshuffle my work load appropriately. Use your body efficiently but wisely.

Don't overschedule. You'll get exhausted and break down. Not the thing to do. If you wake up in the morning with the "how am I going to get through this" feeling, you've gone too far. Start dumping. When children are involved in your schedule, you can't always count on things happening when they should. If you're booked too tight, you'll only go nuts, and make the children nuts, by trying to conform to your list. Give yourself contingency time. It's one of the prices of children.

Make sure you're covered by someone competent when you know you won't be available. Set up a system for car pool, errands, or mother work so you or a substitute can get things done effectively and you needn't take time from business to worry further. Make sure every activity in your schedule and the children's is covered.

Bringing In Professional Help

Most of us are reluctant to ask for help when we suspect we are going to need it. We'll do our best, perhaps try and try, and then admit failure and finally ask for help. We're particularly stubborn about tasks we think we should be able to do without help.

I used to think my inability to cope with work and a child was clearly my fault! I was not organized enough; I wasn't eating properly so I didn't have enough stamina —whatever I couldn't accomplish or was hard for me I blamed on myself. I was sure everyone else was doing just fine. I didn't know that I was drowning and should have called for help from the first day.

A maid is the first kind of help each stepparent should consider. Whatever you can afford, be it for one day or every day, if you need help and a maid can give you that help, it's worth thinking about ahead of time. Many women who work full time have maids or housekeepers to help with the children. Often, their salary is not more than the maid's, and that leaves little profit—save the knowledge that they're doing what they want.

When you hear that giant scream of help welling up inside your stomach, shout out and ask your husband for help. Maybe the family can take over some of your burdens. Maybe you can get a college student in exchange for room and board. Maybe it's time for a housekeeper. The time these things should be done is when you first feel that awful feeling; only you can open your mouth and do something about it.

If you need more complete help than a girl who comes in to clean and iron on Wednesdays and Saturdays, you may need a nanny or governess for the children. (If you have full-time care of children who need constant adult care, but you yourself are unwilling to give up your job, a nanny is a reasonable solution. You can hire a nanny for only a month.)

The idea is to get the help *before* you think you're going to lose your mind. You will have plenty of warning signs: if you choose to ignore them, you're only asking for trouble.

If you don't need a maid, maybe you need a shrink. I did. I went to a family therapist who only dealt with families in crisis.

I spent my first sessions angrily denying that I was crazy or that I needed help. After I worked through that stage, I was able to walk in and spend my hour ranting and raving about the hurts and horrors of stepmotherhood. It lifted a tremendous burden off of Mike, who no longer had to share my anger, and I was able to see better what was really happening to me. The extent of Amy's control over our lives became more clear and I was able to reach out and grab my life back. Not without a lot of trouble, I might add, but I did eventually become the victor. Within six months (and $500) I was able to understand the problems and handle them effectively. It was the best money I ever spent.

As stepparents we have little place in society to show our true feelings. Even while we are plotting to murder the kids, we must act like we love and want them in our lives. We try to act civilized toward a former spouse and reject outright hair pulling, scratching, punching and bludgeoning despite occasional feelings to the contrary. So stepparents, more than any other kind of parents, are a bundle of frustrations. They need someone to help them shout it out and a therapist is a wonderful solution.

Every city in this country has some kind of mental health program scaled to fit your income. In many cases, there are free programs for those who cannot afford to pay. Stepparents as an angry minority are just beginning to raise their voices and psychologists and family therapists are responding.

If there is no therapist you can afford or no program suitable to your needs, form your own rap session. Because stepfathers and stepmothers have different types of problems, it's better to separate your group according to sex—but not imperative. With one in every three marriages ending in divorce, you won't have trouble putting together such a group. Ask your spiritual leader for help in forming the group or you can advertise.

Being a working stepparent can be more than any fragile human can deal with. Don't be embarrassed by being human. Bring in all the help you can.

What Your Job Can Buy For You

Your job can buy you a number of things you may have never thought about before. Besides the disposable income that you may choose to use for nanny, maid, or mental health, jobs often have benefits for employees and their children that singles are unaware of. As a single person, you probably never checked the company's family health plans—whichever is better should carry the family, the whole family. Most divorce agreements require the noncustodial parent to provide some kind of medical and dental care, maybe even pay for the child's therapist. A good health plan will have dental and psychiatric benefits as well as the usual medical ones. Check it out. Even if they're step not natural children, they *can* go on your health plan.

Your job might also have family-oriented sports events, such as its own bowling, baseball, or softball teams. While you personally may have shunned these activities, you may find them great for your stepchildren—if only as a way for them to meet other children.

Many companies have travel packages available for employees and their families only. Airlines give large discounts to their employees and families, and many large corporations arrange special trips to vacation spots—often Disneyland or Disneyworld or places where you would like to take children. Even if you are a noncustodial parent, your stepchildren qualify as part of your family.

Ask about medical insurance, travel, and specific benefits for a family. The larger the company and bigger its position in the community, the more benefits it has for its employees and their families. Find out.

Your job might also have its own special prerequisites that can help you out, or allow you special tax deductions that you don't know about. My current job as a reporter allows me to hire child care tax free, something I just found out this year. (The laws do change.) My employer will let me put baby-sitting fees on my expense account if I am required to cover a story at night and thus hire a baby-sitter. (But they will not let me write off kitty care if I have to go out of town and board my cats with the vet.)

If you are a secretary in a firm and the boss asks you to greet guests at an office cocktail party, or perform any duties that cause you expense for care of your stepchildren, your office should pay for them. Find out.

You may also get product benefits if you work for a company that makes something.

The electronics company you work for may supply Sony and have a deal wherein you can buy Sony products at cost. This can benefit your stepchildren as well as yourself. Ask around, see what your peers can get their kids through the office. Stepchildren should get the same privileges.

Involving Your Kids In Your Work

Most kids are interested in what their parents do at work. What you do—or did today—is a quick and easy road to conversation and establishing your own identity, so it behooves a stepparent to advise the stepkids as to what he does and involve them in some understanding of that work. Some jobs are obviously more interesting to kids than others, some are more visual than others and lend themselves to field trips or a day at the office on a Saturday.

Involving your kids in your work, in even a limited way, is a very real way of making a connection with them and establishing yourself as a real person with a distinct personality and job to fulfill. Perhaps when they see the intricacies of your job they will have more respect for you.

Many people are actually able to put their children and stepchildren to work for them in a real capacity—and are even able to pay them for services rendered. You may be able to establish your authority through a work situation when you were unable to get their attention at home. One stepmother I know set up her eldest stepson (who was old enough to drive and cause trouble with the younger kids) in a family business wherein she paid him for running errands and driving car pool. She treated him with great respect and reinforced his ego by telling him how she counted on him. He, in turn, was never late, and turned his anger and frustration into a bank account. She paid him the going chauffeur rate, and while he never had enough to become independent, he did have spending money and was glad for some freedom. He also liked being treated like a responsible adult and responded to his stepmother's trust in him.

Most children will help out when you explain your needs to them. Goal accomplishment is something even your children understand. You can explain that because you have some work to get done and can't make dinner, they are helping you out at the office by making dinner with their father. Unless your stepchildren are terribly antagonistic, they will be glad to help you out with your work. Don't forget to reward them to show your appreciation.

Bringing A Child To Work With You

In most circles it's considered unprofessional to bring your children to work with you. Yet all of us have to do it some time or another. Once or twice everyone in the office will smile benevolently at you and nod with understanding. More than that, they want to know where you get your nerve.

Stepparents who have not properly prepared something to do with their kids have to take them to the office. I took Amy to work with me for two summers, and still take her on story assignments sometimes. I get angry having to do it, yet it often makes the most sense.

If you're caught without plans for the kids' day and can't get a baby-sitter:

• Try to have a light day so you can leave the office early or won't be disturbed when the kids interrupt your work every half-hour.

• Find something for them to do at the office: run to the editors; sharpen pencils; organize the stockroom; run the Xerox machine. Put them to work in any menial job they are capable of without angering anyone in the office.

• Pay them for their services and reinforce good work verbally.

• Bring along a supply of toys, coloring books, and games to keep them occupied.

• Plan a special lunch. Even if it's in the cafeteria like the grown-ups or at your desk, make it appear important. It will help break up the day.

• Thank your work mates for their help and cooperation. If they didn't help and you thank them anyway, they'll get the point.

Alternatives To Bringing Children To Work

People usually have to bring their children to work with them because they have not taken the time to prepare ahead and realize that they can do something they can afford with the kids and allow everyone some freedom. If you can't afford a nanny, housekeeper, or full-day baby-sitter, don't worry, few other people can either.

Day-care centers were created for working parents. They open early in the morning and keep your child all day with supervised care, play, and nap times and—exactly what your child needs—other children. Find a day-care center either through friends' recommendations or the yellow pages. If you're not happy with the caliber or the price of your findings, create your own on a small enough scale to not need licensing. Hire a teacher or camp counselor type to care for children of your friends—either alternating homes or backyards throughout the week. One woman I know set up what she called The Mommy Brigade. She and four friends arranged to work four days a week. Each was then a full-time mommy to the five children involved. She started out early in the morning and was exhausted at night, but only had to do it once a week and knew her children were well taken care of and stimulated.

For summers, there are day camps and "spend the night" camps. Check your local Y and the yellow pages. Usually Y camps are in one-week sessions so its easy to commit for a short period of time. You have to book ahead in peak summer periods. Many Y's have day-care centers or after-school programs during the school year.

Extended school programs are offered at some schools in which the students can stay after class and study, use the library, play in the playground, and have some supervision. Ask at your child's school or a neighborhood school.

What To Try Giving Up

Mother told you you couldn't have everything. Even if you didn't believe her then, now that you're a working stepparent you obviously see the wisdom of her cliches. Mother was right.

Life is a matter of priorities, so there are some things you'll just have to give up. Try some of these shortcuts and see if you gain more time for the things that are important to you:

• Give up breakfast at home. Have you ever figured out how long it takes you to make and eat a full, not to mention leisurely, breakfast? While the family breakfast may be a ritual prescribed out of "Father Knows Best," your family may hold together very well if they fend for themselves—or if someone else makes their breakfast. You, the working parent, can dash out the door ordering breakfast up to your desk, bringing it in from the coffee shop across the street, or pulling it out of your refrigerator for eating at your convenience once in the office. Yogurt with wheat germ, fresh fruit and tea with honey is a pretty good breakfast, and it's easy to pack up and quick to eat—neat too.

• Quit cooking. You work a hard day at the office. He works a hard day at the office. Who could even consider shredding lettuce for a salad? Forget it. Have cold meals, buy frozen gourmet, hire a cook, or go out to eat. The kids will love it; so will you.

• Stop shopping at several grocery stores to get the best prices. Your time is too valuable now. What you pay in extra pennies by missing the neighborhood bargains will come back to you in dollars of time and energy saved by one-stop shopping. Also shop in big hauls rather than small for the same reasons.

• Give up one lunch hour a week for errands. Whatever you do on your lunchtime, be it eat with the girls, grade papers, or study the stock exchange—give it up for one day a week and do all the dumb things that can ruin a Saturday or put you over the edge when done after work. Go to the cleaner, shoemaker, watch repair; buy camp clothes. You truly can conquer the world in an hour.

• Have you thought of giving up your salary? Lots of working parents do do it. Almost the entire salary goes to a nanny or a housekeeper or someone to take over the mother work and make life more fun. It's all a matter of priorities.

• Be sure you give up any bad eating and poor exercise habits you have: stamina will improve if you exercise regularly and eat foods that are good for you. If you have sick children in your house, you can't afford to catch what they've got—eat well and take vitamins. Never give up caring for yourself.

The Baby-sitter Solution

If you only need part-time help in raising your step-children while you work, you may do well to find a baby-sitter. A student who has the same school hours as your kids and who lives in the neighborhood would be ideal.

How to pick a baby-sitter:

• Never hire a baby-sitter you've never met for steady work. Interview her. Try her out for an evening or a weekend. You can't leave your kids with a stranger and not worry about them.

• Check your sitter's references unless you have known the sitter for a long time. If you don't know the sitter, make sure you know her references. Good marks from strangers are meaningless.

• Take some time to talk to the sitter. Observe her (him) in action with your children. Make sure you have similar values and standards. Is your sitter as childish as your children? If so, forget it.

• Define the job to the sitter. Make sure she can handle it. Once you are satisfied with your sitter, you must train him (her) to your satisfaction.

• Take the time to teach someone how you want things done. If it means staying home from work for a day, stay home. No one can read your mind and raise your children to your liking without a few lessons.

• Make sure the sitter is trained for emergencies. Emergency numbers should be by each telephone. Medicine cabinets should be well stocked. The book, "A Sigh Of Relief," or a "How-To" book for emergencies should be easily accessible.

• Pay your baby-sitter according to work exerted. If your kids are monsters, you better pay accordingly, or you'll soon need a new baby-sitter.

• Lay down the rules of the house and voice your expectations. Can the sitter plunk your kids in front of the TV or is she expected to play with the kids? Can she talk on the phone without limit? Are the children to be driven anywhere? Fed? Bathed?

When hiring a teenage baby-sitter you must remember to keep your expectations in line with the age and capabilities of the sitter. If it's not working out, ask yourself if it's because of this individual sitter, or because your needs and expectations are greater than what can be provided.

How To Have Time For Yourself

It's really very simple. You take it.

Having time off is vital to your self esteem. Accepting that you must have your own time will help you schedule it better. You will be able to combine work at the office and work at home better when you're able to slip off for an hour in a hot tub or to sit alone and read magazines and relax. Being alone for an hour a day is the best therapy in the world. Before you go off to spend your bucks finding out why you can't live happily with a full work schedule and a house full of children, make sure you're taking time to yourself. It just may save you $40 an hour with a shrink.

I felt that my original obligation as a stepmother was to be a great mother, which I therefore thought meant being with Amy every second she was awake, pumping her with input. I was reluctant to dump her in front of the television set so I could go off on my own. I thought for sure I'd lose my motherhood badge and get reported to the good fairies of America. Pretty soon they'd send a fairy godmother to investigate my child's case and I'd get a wicked rating. Oh, God, no.

It was so hard for me to work and be a mother at the same time that rather than take time for myself, I constantly cast it away. Who needs to wear makeup? Who needs to wear pantyhose? Who needs to take a bath alone? Pretty soon I was chained to Amy and filled with hate and anger. How did other mothers work and enjoy their children?

Simple: they take baths by themselves; they plunk the kids in front of the television for an hour; they think enough of themselves to take time for their sanity. Here's how to do it:

1. Find the best time to take an hour from your day—a time that will make you appreciate your time off and refresh you for more of the day.

2. Reschedule your days to fit that hour regularly; don't haphazardly fit it in someplace. This is more important than piano practice. Same time every day and I don't want to hear any excuses.

3. Announce the new plan to the entire family. Explain the types of intrusions you will tolerate (fire). Post hours. Get a do-not-disturb sign for your door. Treat transgressors with scorn.

4. Make no exceptions. Pretty soon it's the PTA meeting. Then it's the bake sale. Then it's a little bit of office work you didn't quite get done and this is your only chance to catch up. Take no prisoners. Advance to the firing line. This is between you and your inner-self and you must follow through.

5. Think good thoughts about yourself as an individual. Career and mother work may make you feel like a maniac running a mean race from office to grocery store. Only thinking good thoughts about yourself can overcome the system's injustices. You are worth pampering.

Time For The Two Of You

The first time that Amy came to live with us, Mike and I were rarely alone. We did sleep alone, but I always went to sleep before Amy and never saw Mike until morning. We had no time for sex, no time for secrets and could barely avoid Amy's keen mind—unless we spoke French—a ploy handicapped by my inadequate knowledge of the language (I'm only good at menus). Mike and I used to actually sneak into the bathroom to have a few minutes of privacy.

We were so insecure about ourselves as parents that we truly never once said to Amy: "Look here kid, bug off." It probably would have been very easy—we just never even considered it. We thought that working parents had to spend all their nonworking hours with the children.

By the next visit I was more prepared. I would kidnap Mike as he entered the apartment and announce that Daddy and I are going to have a half hour to ourselves as I whisked him into the bedroom. I had visions of Amy standing at our door with her ear, or eye, to the keyhole wondering what we were saying about her. (Plenty.) We found that the only way to survive her stay was to take time out for ourselves to renew our own relationship. We finally set aside two different times of the day as ours alone, not necessarily for sex, but for just being us: early morning and before dinner.

The announcement of this new policy was not met with glee. Amy thought it a mean, dirty trick and an obvious sign that we didn't love her any more and didn't want her. She even complained to her mother (we were outraged) that the only time I wanted to be with Daddy was when she came to visit. Her mother immediately accused me of infantile jealousy that was inexcusable in a twenty-eight-year-old woman. But we continued to take time out for ourselves. Our time together became a pivotal priority in keeping our marriage together.

Working parents suffer a terrible amount of guilt and are always trying to work out better ways of fulfilling themselves as workers and parents—they want it all, but not finding enough time for it all, feel guilty if they aren't constantly available for their children.

Working stepparents and part-time parents have even less time to be with the kids if they are noncustodial parents. They must combine the rigors of their work with a quality, instead of a quantity, approach to childraising.

It's easy for the stepparent to feel the "them against me" syndrome as the original members of the family form their weekend alliances. It's easy for the stepparent to go from a hard day at the office to a hard day as social coordinator for a guilty parent with no emotional rewards. Time alone for two mates when the children are around is not something they plan for. Wrongly so.

Reconsidering What You Are About To Tackle

Very few stepmothers take time to think out what will happen to them when they combine *their* jobs with *his* children. If the combination seems dangerous, they ignore the possibilities and enter the arena trying to make the best of it. There is little time spent wondering if it's going to work out or if there is an alternative to making it work out.

If your life is full enough without someone else's children, you don't have to accept them in your life. And you certainly don't have to give up your life-style to accomodate the kids. A baby-sitter for the kids, dinners out, and a maid to clean up are all viable alternatives making life easier to cope with—especially if you work full time.

Don't fall into the fantasy trap of thinking you can do it better, that if so and so can be a working mother so can you or that you can one up anyone, let alone that bitch who was married to your husband. Sometimes the investment isn't worth it. Careful and considerable thought on whether you can maintain your career and still be a part-time parent is essential. And you shouldn't be embarrassed to quit before you begin.

Don't be a martyr thinking it will buy you happiness. It won't. Don't try to show your love for your husband by taking on the duties of super stepmom when you're not up to them. Be honest with yourself and stay yourself. Your marriage will last—and so will your health.

6.
How To Talk
And Think Like
A Parent

How To Talk And Think
Like A Parent

I've heard it said that immediately following the birth of
your first child, while the baby is still being sponged,
weighed, and measured, an orderly brings the new mother
an extra set of eyes for the back of her head and installs
them free of charge. While this system has worked quite
well over the years, it has left instant mommies, well, in the
dark. I understand that sooner or later a deal will be made
with City Hall, so that stepparents may also receive their
extra set of eyes when they welcome their new children to
the family.

When we were married, the state of Texas gave us a

plastic bag filled with all the necessities in beginning our lives together—a package of Rolaids, some Listerine, a sample of new Bounce, some Phillip's tablets (strawberry), a miniature-sized can of Glade, and a small but handy box of Kleenex. But no eyes. (Even in Texas!) Perhaps if we had brought our daughter to the courthouse with us, we would have been more lucky.

But then, besides the eyes, I would have liked to have a dictionary of mommy. Mommy, like any other occupation, has its own lingo. That's how you can tell the insiders from the outsiders; the real mommies from the fake mommies. It's like the "rag" business or the music business—they all have their own special lingo. Watch enough cop shows and you get to learn street talk. Same with mommy. Nothing sticks out worse than a parent who doesn't know his stuff.

Of course, you can never totally win, no matter what your fluency. Once you start passing that child off as your own there's going to be something you don't know that will make you look like a real idiot. What mother wouldn't know when her child's birthday was? The name of her kid's school? When she had her last tetanus shot?

I had a terribly embarrassing time once when I called the balloon man to order some "Happy Birthday Amy" balloons for our daughter.

"And when is her birthday?" asked the balloon man. "I think the balloons should have the date on them."

Oh, no! No date. I was horrified. I mean, I knew her birthday was some time soon and it was time to get the balloons made and mailed off—but I didn't know the exact date. (I do now.) But I had called her my daughter and now I was a mommy.

I also suffered a little bit of panic the day she asked me to tell her a story. My god! A story? I just didn't have any stories in mind.

Do you admit that you don't know any good stories and that you can barely remember the traditional ones? Do you fake it? And you dare to call yourself a mommy. Honestly . . .

Parenthood is a very elite club, and you've really got to know the territory to be accepted. Before you had children and you visited with friends who already had children (their own children), you knew it was there, didn't you? That terrible gap of silence. That disdain. You were disdainful of her because she was trapped with two young children and all she wanted to talk about was how hard it is to find a decent school system these days. She looked at you crookedly because you were running around with older men and generally wasting your life when you could settle down and be a real person and do something worthwhile. You had nothing to talk about. Or whatever she was talking about bored you. You just didn't speak the same language.

Your fluency in Parent (a Romance language?) depends on how often you have children around you, how much younger your own siblings are, how recently you were with them, and how many real parents you hang out with. Besides speaking Parent, there's thinking Parent—the nonverbal category is just as important. I happened to flunk my first test in nonverbal Parent.

My husband, our daughter, and I were taking a cab through Central Park and the driver hit a bump while speeding around a curve. I grabbed the car strap. My husband threw his arm out across his daughter to stop her from falling forward. I was very embarrassed and refused to look him straight in the face all day. But I got him back the next day when I learned the words "day-care center."

If your inherited child is past three, words like "pabulum" and "pottie seat" have passed you by. You're into the big stuff like "training wheels," "flame retardant," **"6-X"** and "pooh-pooh."

How To Talk To A Child

People who do not have regular contact with children are often frightened of talking to kids. "I don't know what to say to a child" is everyone's most common complaint. You'd think that children speak a foreign language. They do not. If you remember two simple rules about addressing children, you will never have trouble again—and probably never fear their company again.

1. Never talk down to a child or talk to him as if he were a child. Treat children as if they were linguistically equal (whenever feasible) and you'll get a better response. Do not talk baby talk even to infants.

2. Remember that children don't have the same rules of reality adults do, so hang loose. Consider subjects an adult would think nonsense. Children appreciate the ridiculous as well as the sublime. You can always make friends with a child by discussing the ridiculous.

Not every child, or every adult, is a talker. If you can only get yeses and nos and shrugs of the shoulders, you shouldn't give up. It takes time to warm up to a stranger. If the child feels hostile toward you, you will know it. Otherwise, maybe words aren't necessary. No matter how well you get the child talking, do remember that you will never be able to sustain days of conversation with a child. I once took Amy for a five-day trip to San Francisco and although we had a wonderful time, meal time was incredibly bleak. Amy and I had nothing to say to each other. If you're not talking about something you are involved in doing, or asking about school and friends, there might not be much to talk about. There probably shouldn't be, but you should be prepared for the inevitable.

One of my husband's most horrible frustrations was trying to communicate with his daughter on the telephone when we lived in New York. They would both say "Hi," then he would ask her a variety of questions like "How's school?" and "How're your friends?" She answered everything with "Fine." That was it. If you didn't have a list of questions or a topic to talk to her about, you were finished in thirty seconds and depressed for three days. Young children are no good on the phone and may not be great conversationalists in person. Give yourself a break by accepting this up front.

Look for conversation openers in the reference chapter of this book, or try a few of these:

• Do you know any knock-knock jokes?

• Hey, did you hear that it's going to be against the law to go to school?

• Do you think Pippi Longstocking will ever get elected president?

• Think the Angels (Mets, Dodgers, etc.) have a chance?

If desperate, you can always ask that old standby:

• Cat got your tongue? What kind of cat was it?

How To Win A Child's Respect

First of all, you can't do it with bribery. You may think you can; it may even appear as if you are succeeding, but children who are being bribed know it, and they also know how to pull the manipulative strings. You will never have the respect of a child you are bribing, so forget it right away. You can only get respect by winning it. And you win a child much the same way you win an adult—slowly and carefully.

• Never treat a child like a child and certainly not like a child of a younger age.

• Treat a child with respect and show him you ask the same from him.

• Never make fun of the child or cause him embarrassment. A joke at his expense will also be at yours.

• Show him you don't need his approval, that you are your own person. Trying too hard lays the ground work for manipulative behavior and loss of respect. Play hard to get.

• Discipline when necessary. If you have no authority, you have no respect.

How to Discipline
Someone Else's Children

Just like you would discipline your own. Stepparents without the authority to discipline have no real place in the family: they can be manipulated, stepped on, and eliminated from the power pyramid. Even if the stepparent resorts to the trusty "Wait-till-your-father-(mother)-comes-home" routine, discipline should be faced by both adults. If the natural parent thinks that no discipline is indicated, or backs the child rather than the stepparent, the stepparent will have a very unhappy life in this family.

If the children are of an age or size at which it is physically impossible to discipline them, the stepparent must have the backing of the natural parent in handing out restrictions and suggesting when discipline is necessary.

When planning to discipline a stepchild, ask yourself these questions:

• Am I being rational? A stepchild may anger you beyond the limits of normal behavior. Analyze the crime, the punishment, and your reaction before you act.

• Does the punishment fit the crime? You cannot order the firing squad up at dawn for failure to empty the kitty litter. It's a union rule. Don't punish inconsequential crimes with heavy-duty artillery.

• Are you being consistent? The same crime can't be a felony some days and a misdemeanor on others. Several children cannot have varying punishments for the same act. Step and natural children must always be treated alike.

How To Child-proof Your Home

If you have no children in your household, you're in for a big surprise: children can get into *everything*, and accidental deaths lay in every room of your home or apartment. Even if his kids just come to visit you on rare occasion, you can't be too safe. Follow these safety tips:

• Lock your medicine cabinets.

• Don't store anything but food in food containers.

• Never keep medicine (even aspirin or cough drops) out, or in your handbag.

• Make sure all appliances and machinery cannot be turned on by the children.

• If you have a refrigerator or freezer outside the kitchen, make sure it's locked and the key is hidden. Or take the door or top off.

• Make sure plastic bags and dry-cleaning bags are not accessible.

• Keep stairs and steps blockaded with guard rails or fences.

• Use child-proof hinges (available at dime and hardware stores) on all kitchen cabinets and especially where all cleaning supplies are.

• Never leave a child alone in a room in which you are using a cleaning product, cooking, or using an electrical appliance.

• Make sure all windows are covered with screens or iron grills that cannot be pushed out.

• Remember to always turn handles of pots and pans inward so a grasping hand cannot reach them.

• If you have a swimming pool, make sure it is child-proof.

• Survey your home with the eyes of a child—look at objects his height, explore what can be eaten, inhaled, poured over, played with, and ignited.

Children under the age of five cannot tell the difference between what's dangerous and what isn't. They certainly don't know right from wrong. And they may not heed just one "no."

How To Be Informed
About Parent Stuff

If you have no children of your own, or yours are over the age of twenty-five, you may be interested in catching up on the parenting industry that has begun to bloom. Every spring and fall new books on the latest methods of child raising come into the stores. And almost every woman's magazine has a special page dedicated to the latest news of interest to parents only. It's possible you subscribe to these magazines and are thumbing past their mothering pages, or—if you were a single girl until recently—have not begun to read this type of magazine. Obviously, *Cosmopolitan* has nothing in it about child raising. But a subscription to *Redbook* or *McCall's* may prove a worthwhile investment.

If the books and magazines now available don't satiate your quest for knowledge, talk to your pediatrician. He will tell you how to write for several free booklets on topics of your choice.

How To Find Another Mother

Mothers share a set of problems indicative of the breed. *If you've never been a mother before,* you might not have any friends who are mothers and would like to find at least one with whom to share your problems.

Ask at your office. There's probably a number of women the same age you are who are mothers who may not be in your circle because you never had anything in common before. Easy accessibility to your mother source is vital, so check where you work first.

Your neighborhood. Follow some kids home one night and introduce yourself to their mother. Explain your problems (not at dinner time), your need for someone to touch base with. She'll probably be glad to help out or recommend someone else in the neighborhood who might have children the same age as yours.

Call your own mother. She will be of some help even though she probably can't remember much and things have changed considerably since her children were the age yours are now. She's a good place to start. If you live in the same town, she will have peers with children your age and perhaps they have children.

Old friends. Trace your old friends from high school or college you have lost track of and find out what they're doing and if they have children. I often call a high school chum for mother information because her daughter is a year older than Amy. We weren't even very good friends in high school, but she's been very helpful now.

How To Find Someone To Answer Even Your Dumbest Questions

When I first started having child-raising questions; I immediately called my mother. Amy had diarrhea but didn't appear to be seriously sick. What should or shouldn't she be eating? Would scraping the peel of an apple really do any good? My mother, to my sheer amazement, told me she couldn't remember.

I had no other friends with children. I didn't think I needed to bother a doctor. What to do? Call the home economics department of a local college or university. Whether it's how to take a child's temperature, or how to cook a pot roast, they know the answer. Or they'll find it out for you.

How To Say No

It's easy. You just put your lips together and blow. The thing about saying "no" that instant parents seldom realize is how little impact—especially immediate impact—the word really has. You can't summon up your courage, spit out the word "no," and think you're done. "No" is heard so often in so many different ways by children that they seldom absorb it—or even hear it—the first few times.

You must say "no" in order to protect your own freedoms and a child's well-being. You must repeatedly say "no" if you believe in what you're saying.

How To Buy Clothes For A Child

If you know nothing about the child you are buying clothes for and have no idea of his or her sizes, use the common rule devised when children's sizes were introduced: the child wears his age. Also remember that too big is better than too small. If you've heard that the child is large (or small) for his age, adjust your thinking accordingly. Avoid bargain clothes or unlabeled merchandise because they probably don't run true to size. Remember to check the stretch in the neck of T-shirts to make sure they will go over your child's head. If it's hard to get into, the child won't want to wear it. Never buy clothes that need to be ironed or dry cleaned or look like they will run—unless the clothes are for a special occasion and you don't mind the cleaning bill. Remember to check closures for ease in dressing. Does a dress have a back zipper that a child couldn't possibly do herself, making the dress less practical than one that wraps in the front? The older the child, the more he wants to dress himself. Closures that are beyond his ability may be frustrating and will color his feelings about the garment. "Is it comfortable?" is what a child really cares about first, then, "Can I get into it myself?" Stiff fabrics or itchy fabrics will not be met with zeal, while soft and cuddly ones will be greatly appreciated. Some children become "clothes horses," others never do. A lot of that is environmental conditioning, while some is peer pressure. The older the child, though, the more interest usually displayed in fashion.

How To Make Cinnamon Toast

Believe it or not, there's a right way and a wrong way to make cinnamon toast, and anyone masquerading as a parent will quickly be found out should he or she err.

The Wrong Way To Make Cinnamon Toast. Toast the bread, butter it quickly while it's hot, sprinkle cinnamon and sugar mixture on top, serve immediately.

The Right Way To Make Cinnamon Toast. Toast the bread. Butter and sprinkle with cinnamon-sugar mixture. (Which you already have mixed together.) Place in broiler or oven until crisp. Serve.

Congratulations, now you are *really* a parent. Tomorrow you advance to hot chocolate.

How To Be Prepared For Parenting

The Parent Bag is a stepparent's, part-time parent's, and grandparent's most essential aid, because it houses everything that might be needed while the parent is on duty. Real mothers always have these tools on hand, but those who snap back and forth between two roles can rely on the Parent Bag as the one place that keeps most everything needed. The best Parent Bag is a good-sized tote bag—not too large because you do have to carry it around with you. Probably not too feminine either, as you will be asking your husband to carry it for you a lot. Include:

- Safety pins
- Kleenex
- Camera and flash cubes
- Band-Aids
- Life Savers or sugar-free gum

• Coloring book plus crayons, or drawing paper with crayons

• Great book that you can read to your child

• Book you child loves to read to you. (Children love repetition; they don't care if they've read the book thirty times before.)

• Small sewing kit

• A & D ointment or some other soothing cure-all

• Rubber bands, barrettes, brush, comb, hair ribbons

• Wash 'n' Dries, Wet Ones, or some kind of towel-lette

• Clean pair of socks

• Baby aspirin

• Bathing suit (if it's summer—you'd be surprised how many impromptu swimming events pop up)

• Sweater (if it's winter, fall or early spring)

How To Drive
With Children In The Car

Amy and I have a running battle in the car. She likes to sit in the front seat and put her legs against the dashboard. I have explained to her in a rational manner that if I stop short, or if we are in an accident, both her legs will break immediately, probably in several places. I have even demonstrated (more or less) what will happen. No response. Driving with Amy became a difficult chore. I was forced to raise my voice, threaten her, and lose my cool.

Yet there are several rules of car safety that need to be enforced when you have children in your life:

• No tickling the driver.

• In fact, no bothering the driver in any manner whatsoever.

● No excessive screaming, shouting, hitting, hair pulling, seat hopping, or rolling around by other members of the moving car.

● Seat belts for everyone.

● No playing with sharp objects or pointed objects. This includes drinking from a cup with a straw in a moving vehicle.

● No parts of the body out the window at any time.

● No music the driver doesn't approve of.

● No extension of limbs into potentially hazardous pressure points: legs on dashboard, etc. No sleeping on back window shelf, if your car has one.

How to Bathe a Child

For some reason, children universally hate to bathe. They will swear they just bathed yesterday, calmly explain that whatever dirt you find on them isn't really dirt, and insist that a bath is unnecessary. If it weren't so funny, it would be boring. At various stages of their childhood, children will actually enjoy their baths once they are in progress. At other ages the whole process is a terrible struggle. The essence of parenthood always seems to distill down to a power struggle over bathing.

So consider these hints:

● If you can't get the kids to bathe, let your spouse do it.

● If the child is the same sex as you, or if you're fully liberated, take the kid in the bath or shower with you. Or send them in in pairs while you supervise from the sidelines.

● Make bathing a treat. Try scented bubble baths, shaped and scented soaps, matching shower caps, terry cloth bath mitts, etc. There are even finger paints that are bath gels.

• Survey the bathing situation from your child's size and height. Maybe there's a good reason why he hates bathing. Is the tub easy to get in and out of? Is it slippery? Dangerous? Does the shampoo burn his eyes? Is the water too hot?

When bathing a child—or children—remember to never leave them unsupervised. Ignore the phone if it rings. Avoid the doorbell. The younger the child, the greater chance of accidents.

How To Wash A Child's Hair

For some reason, children are unanimously opposed to washing their hair and consider it a real drag—even at the rate of once a week. Realize this, and accept it. Your child may even lie about the last time he washed his hair to get out of doing it at your home. I find the old bend-your-head-in-the-sink-and-we'll-rub-a-dub-dub very uncomfortable for little girls and recommend you send them to the shower, even if you have to shower together or stand in the steam to supervise.

Keep shampoos that can get in the eyes without causing tears (Johnson's Baby Shampoo, but there are others, too) and, if available, get a "fun" shampoo that doesn't make the eyes tear and is scented and well-packaged. Showering together is the simplest way to attack the problem—you can control the whole job and do the rub and dubbing yourself to make sure she's clean. I wouldn't trust a child under the age of ten to do a thorough job without supervision. Most beauticians say adults don't know how to wash their own hair, so you can imagine what a child will do. If she has long hair, try No More Tangles or some creme rinse, otherwise she might accuse you of trying to kill her when you pull out the snarls . . . and she may threaten to tell her mommy.

Boys? Send them to the showers. No sissy brand shampoos. Introduce conditioners at an early enough age and they will take. If dad thinks the appearance of his hair is important, his attitude will transfer to his son.

How To Eat Out With Children

Eating out with children requires a delicate frame of mind. You must be prepared for trouble from the restaurant staff, the strangers coincidentally dining in the same restaurant, and your children. My biggest shock in dining out with Amy is that restaurants discriminate against children. Unless known as a family restaurant, they will indeed send you to Siberia.

Most children are on their best behavior when they go out to restaurants. Amy was as well-behaved as any adult when she was seven and Mike and I often chose restaurants with fancy decors we thought she'd enjoy. Most of them did not appreciate the thought.

If you are not going to a family-oriented restaurant, remember to bring something for a child to sit on if he is too small to sit at a table without a high seat. The maitre d' will reluctantly lend you his phone book, but only with a disdainful glance. Don't ask for child-sized portions if they aren't listed on the menu—more scorn. Remember not to go any place so fancy that it won't have what the child likes to eat. My husband tells of eating hamburgers for lunch and dinner on a trip throughout Canada. Accept the fact that kids have weird eating habits and be prepared for them.

If your children are young, bothersome, or noisy, give some thought to where you will be seated. Complaints from your fellow diners will irritate you, even if they are justified. It's wise to let the maitre d' know you have children when you make a reservation in a fancy restaurant, and wise for you to accept the fact that you probably won't be seated at table number one—unless your child is Tatum O'Neal.

If you are dining late, feed the kids before you go out. Then you won't get any whining about hunger pains. Let them order an hors d'oeuvre for dinner or something light. Don't be surprised if they fill up on crackers because they are so hungry and then have no room for the expensive dinner that is brought to them. Even if you kill them then and there, you still have to pay for the dinner. Don't forget about doggie bags for uneaten food.

It helps to take your children to a restaurant where you are known so you will get special attention and any childish indiscretions may be looked past. Also, don't forget that at different ages in their lives children are more ready for different types of restaurants.

How To Feed
Someone Else's Children

Children are incredibly prejudiced about food. Most have their pet favorites and seldom desire to increase their repertoire. Don't be surprised if your stepchild seems to subsist solely on hamburger and French fries, spaghetti or fried chicken—or only those four. Few mothers will cater to their child's eating demands by making separate meals. Should you choose to do this, it's your business. Most people announce that this is dinner, eat it or go hungry. Maybe next time he'll eat it. Children respond best to foods they know: from home, school, or trusted restaurants. Foreign foods and fancy foods may have difficulty in being accepted. Children are a little more susceptible to new dishes when introduced in another person's home (as the stepparent, you're family, not another person) because children will try not to be rude and will taste. You may have been pushing Chinese food for months with no success when your child will burst home with enthusiasm for Chinese dishes he ate with a friend's family. There is no logic to children and what they choose to eat. However, they may choose to not eat something you yourself will not eat because their dislike is reinforced. Tell a child to eat tomatoes when you insist you don't like tomatoes and you won't get too far.

In our family, we find anticipation helps build interest in a new taste. Sometimes we tell Amy we hope she doesn't like something so there will be more for us. Guaranteed she'll love it.

When you take your child to a restaurant be prepared for his ordering whatever favorite he's keen on at that time in his life. For years he may only eat peanut butter and jelly.

How To Make Travel Arrangements For A Child

Airlines have a number of privileges for children that you may not be aware of. For example, if your child travels alone, you may pay full fare; if he travels with an adult, and is under age eleven, he goes for a reduced fare, usually half.

There are also family rates and special prices for students, which include children over eleven. Ask your travel agent or airlines every time you travel. Travel has become such a competitive business that prices are always changing... ask again for every trip you book.

Parents traveling with young children and children traveling alone may board the aircraft before all the other passengers and will be helped on board by crew members and made comfortable before the mob starts pouring on to the plane. Advise the airlines that you are traveling with young children.

If you are a large family traveling together, especially on well-booked flights, call your airline the day before your flight and explain that you need seven seats across for your family members. They will block them out in advance.

If you are putting children on a plane for a flight by themselves, you are allowed to board the plane and get the child settled. Don't let anyone tell you differently. You will, of course, have to go through all the security checks normal passengers are confronted with. You can also ask the crew to place your child or children with other children traveling with adults.

Be prepared to sign a release for lone travelers.

If your child is a picky eater, pack a meal for him. You can also order a kosher or vegetarian meal, which may be better than the usual plane fare, but there is no promise. Especially on long flights, it's best to send your children with a lunch box of favorites. Also make sure the kids have money for movies on the plane.

If you are traveling by car with children, make sure there are plenty of in-car games to play. Keep a cassette recorder with music and stories so you won't feel obligated to be their only source of entertainment. Remember that children don't have the same amount of bladder control as adults.

Buses, trains, sight-seeing vehicles, and public transportation all have special prices for children. Ask about them. Also learn the cutoff ages. I let Amy be six for two years before I had to pay full fare on the subway ... and it hasn't bothered my conscience at all.

When planning a family vacation, besides asking about children's fares, inquire about complete child packages. Some places brag about letting your kids stay for free. (Honest.) Other places have special arrangements for children and provide you with sitters and recreation for children. My favorite of all is the Club Mediterranee which, at some clubs, not all, has a separate arrangement for your children. You pay one flat price for each family member and get room and meals and all activities: it's like putting the kids in camp but you're still all in the same place having a great time. A vacation like that frees the adults from having to devote themselves to the kids. It's worth every cent.

All the big Las Vegas hotels have day-care centers, so your youngsters could have the time of their lives while you gamble away their child support. The more a resort wants customers, the more special arrangements for children.

How To Get A Baby-sitter

Most parents like to have baby-sitters until the child, or the oldest child, is about thirteen years old. Children start showing some independence in this area at about age eleven, and time of day, proximity of neighbors, and duration of your absence all come to bear in deciding if you need a baby-sitter or not. Most baby-sitters get a dollar an hour, but rates change with the locale, so agree on the price beforehand. You should pick up and deliver the sitter, or arrange for cab fare if you don't have a car. Be very explicit with the baby-sitter about what your expectations are: no talking on the phone, no snacks, no friends over, or whatever. You should have posted the phone number of police, fire department, ambulance, and the number where you can be reached. Most mothers phone in and check up on the sitter at bedtime, in the guise of saying good night to their child. Baby-sitters are rarely tipped, but many charge extra for time after midnight. If you have a baby-sitter you and the children are particularly fond of, you might want to remember her at Christmas time, etc.

How to find a baby-sitter:

• Ask a friend or neighbor who has children.

• There are agencies with scads of little old ladies who do baby-sitting.

• Kids start baby-sitting when they're about thirteen and usually work until they go away to college. If your neighborhood or apartment building has teenagers who do baby-sitting, talk to a few of them.

• Run an ad in the local paper: i.e., "Occasional mother needs occasional baby-sitter, please have references."

A mommy joke: Any reference to a new baby-sitter and the condition of your home when you return is funny to other mothers.

How To Pick A Day Camp Or Day-care Center

The children are out of school and you are reluctant to give up a day of work to baby-sit—you feel guilty because these children should get all the love and attention you can give them because you see them so rarely, but you'll be damned if you can stay home from work every holiday or every summer just because of the children. Relax. It's okay. If it's summer, this must be day camp. And there's always day care.

Day care is basically day camp, but it's worked around school hours during the school year. It's organized play group so that parents can pick up their children after five without tearing into their day at the office to pick up the kiddies and get them organized. Unfortunately, day-care centers—whether connected with a school or not —usually work on a semester or term type of schedule. If you and your ex-wife (who has the children) live in the same city, you have no problems in maintaining the same day care term. If the use of day care is for your own benefit only, or if you live in different cities, you must make appropriate arrangements. Talk to the people who run the center you're interested in (have more than one interest), explain your circumstances, and estimate how often your child would have need of the center. Offer to make a contribution or to pay partial tuition, based on your calculations.

Day camps also work on a term basis. It will be difficult to get your child into part of a term, but less hard to find day camps with one week sessions.

Feeling guilty? Forget it. Your children belong with other children more than with adults. By the time you are reunited at the dinner table, you will have gotten a good day's work done, your child will have had supervised activities geared to his age group, and playmates of his own age, and, more important, something to talk to you about.

Can't find a day-care center or day camp that meets your needs? Form a co-op with your friends. If five women each agree to give up one day a week and take each other's children, you'll have the same benefits of day care or camp. And possibly more: you can control what your child does, who his playmates are, what he will learn. Your camp counselor might not have the college education your girl friend has, and she surely has more children to deal with. Children in a co-op need not be the exact same age, but should be in the same range so they enjoy the same activities.

How To Make Your Kid Feel Like A Million Bucks

Accomplishment is something that is very important to all of us—especially children. It makes a child feel good to accomplish things himself—without your help. No matter how small the job is, he feels pleased when he's done it himself and it's well done, especially to a parent's satisfaction. Knowing this, don't give your stepchild tasks that are beyond him and then yell or fume when the job wasn't done right. In fact, don't assign a role that is beyond him and will prove frustrating, even if there is no recrimination. Learn your stepchild's capabilities and judge accordingly. Nobody likes to feel like a loser all the time.

Some ways to reinforce your stepchild's accomplishments:

• "That was a *hard* job that no one else wanted. Thank you for tackling it."

• "Boy, are you *brave.* I was terrified of that spider."

• "What an *imaginative* solution."

How To Put The Children To Bed

Know when bedtime is and enforce it. Summer and weekend bedtimes may vary from school bedtimes. Don't trust your child to tell you his true bedtime, ask the natural parent.

Expect that your children will not go gently into that good night. Bedtime is a ritual for most children, especially young ones. Kissing all the animals good night can take one half hour or more.

Don't think it's over so easily. A drink of water or a few trips to the bathroom are common attention getting devices. Put your foot down when you can't take any more. Don't be surprised if tears ensue.

Expect younger children to want night-lights and favorite toys. Remember your "boo banky"?

Do reconsider bedtime as an issue. If the child doesn't have to go to school the next day, you may be merely fighting a power struggle. He'll fall asleep eventually, so you may consider letting him pick his own bedtime and letting yourself out of the usual hassles.

How To Deal With Bed-wetting

Ignore it or be as sympathetic as possible. Stay calm, don't make a big deal out of it. More pressure is the last thing the bed wetter needs. Bed-wetting is almost always psychological; if the situation doesn't improve in a year, get professional help.

How To Deal With Tears

Children cry to communicate their frustrations due to an inability to get what they want or because they hurt. Once you know the child well enough, you will be able to distinguish between the types of tears. At some point you will have to decide if you will be manipulated by tears. Never tease a child about crying. It just makes matters worse.

How To Fool The Kids

If your child is under six years old, you can resort to spelling out words you don't want your child to hear. You can also try pig Latin, which will sustain you until your child is maybe eight. Or you can do what my parents did—speak Yiddish. Unfortunately, most of today's parents don't speak Yiddish. My sister and I are forced to converse in Spanish when we don't want Amy to understand us, and my husband and I have a terrible problem as neither of us speaks the same foreign languages.

I'm for bringing back Yiddish. I think that it should be taught during pregnancy—like the LaMaze method. When you are about to become a parent, you sign up, and a few months later you and your husband (you must take the course together, naturally) graduate with a degree in Parental Yiddish and a copy of Leo Rosten's book *The Joys of Yiddish*. By no means do you have to be Jewish to take this class. Walk around any big city today and you'll find the Irish speak more Yiddish than anyone else—as do your black friends. It's a universal tongue and it should be reused before it dies.

And yes, you can also take the course if you're a conscientious single-on-the-make, or a stepparent.

How To Drive Car Pool

Car pools are the original co-op idea but they only work if a lot of people in the same neighborhood are going to the same place on a regular basis. Should you inherit part of a car pool responsibility from his ex-wife, make sure you know the schedule and when it's your turn. Don't rely on the children to give you instructions on how to get to their homes unless they're over ten.

"You take and I'll pick up" is another driving arrangement that takes only one other partner and is usually easier for stepparents who might not know enough people or have the need for a car pool. Most ten-year-olds are very independent with mass transportation in a city they are used to. Kids who rely on mass transportation to go to school usually know the routes before them. This is, of course, an urban phenomenon. If your child comes from an urban society into your suburban life, he will have more confidence with the idea and availability of public transportation. If it's the other way around, your child will need confidence boosting and lessons in street savvy.

How To Deal With Sexual Role Differentiation

Sexual role differentiation is one of those things you probably never heard of and could care less about, until you become a modern parent. Interesting enough, this is a phenomenon your own mother wasn't interested in, as it has only come into view vis-à-vis the Women's Movement. Sexual role differentiation is when you tell your son not to cry because boys don't cry. I'm not saying teach your son to identify with mommy instead of daddy, I'm simply saying sexual role differentiation is something you'll suddenly run into and might rebel against.

Your rebellion (should you have one) might become more complex when you find your child is raised in two different homes with differing views on the subject. I believe that there's nothing wrong (and a lot right) with boys learning to sew and with girls who know about the insides of a car. As a stepparent you automatically can offer new points of view. This is one area in which you can accomplish a lot.

7.
Is This Child Really Sick?

Amy used to get these terrible headaches. She would be perfectly fine all day long, then suddenly, without any apparent reason, become crippled by a headache. Sometimes the headaches brought on tears, sometimes they were accompanied by stomachaches. They continued without mercy so that Mike and I were quite frantic. Although the headaches would go away an hour or two after they came, we were desperately worried about their regularity and severity. We began to consult a round of specialists. We had Amy's eyes checked. They were perfect. We had a thyroid test done. A blood test. She even had a brain scan. Suppose these terrible headaches were from a tumor! It was frightening, expensive, and frustrating.

I discovered the cause of Amy's headaches quite by

accident and without any medical help. One day Amy threw a tantrum and in her anger spewed all the cliches I remembered from my childhood: she would never speak to us again, one day we would be sorry, she would tell her real mother what we had done to her, etc. I almost started to laugh in remembering my own childhood tantrums and the exact same scenario. Only then I would have proceeded to get good and sick—to make them really sorry they had been so mean to me. And that's how I discovered the cause of Amy's headaches.

There was nothing in the world wrong with our child. Sure, her head really hurt when she said it did and the stomachaches were real enough to her—but she was causing them, to get attention. Amy was full of bull; which is exactly what my father had said to me most of my childhood. How I could have failed to see the facts sooner was frightening, and why no medical doctor or motherly friend ever reminded me of children's attention getting devices is even more frightening.

How to treat Amy and the headaches became the next serious problem. I knew from my childhood that if I told her she was full of bull, as my father had me, it would make matters much worse. She would then have to prove how sick she really was and the whole drama would escalate.

I considered telling her she was seriously ill and thought of playing out a scenario that any child would have loved, but decided I was too cruel. What can you say about a seven-year-old child who loved Walt Disney, the Beatles, and me? I considered my mother's solution—any child who complained of anything of the not very serious to inconsequential level was taken on a tour of a hospital or shoved into the wheelchairs of passersby with a curt, "Now you think you've got problems, Susan?" That usually cured anything.

Alas, I had to be my own person, so I went along with Amy's headaches within a prescribed ritual. I gave her serious attention and told her exactly what was to be done for her headache: she could have four aspirin (children's—she couldn't take adult's and I didn't want to make the punishment too grim), a cold cloth on her head, five minutes worth of sympathy at the bedside, and that was it. If her headache wasn't better by dinner, she would have a dinner of crackers and ginger ale in bed and then go to sleep. It usually worked.

Instant parents are most vulnerable when it comes to their ward's health. Childhood has its own set of occupational hazards and diseases, which adults are aware of but not tuned into simply from lack of necessity. I mean how long ago was it that you were a child? When was the last time that you claimed Bugs Bunny came into your room last night and picked all your scabs while you were asleep? (See, you thought we forgot that one, huh?) When was the last time you got hysterical at the sight of a bumble bee? Have you ever given a rectal thermometer before? An enema? Do you remember what to do for diarrhea?

We are so afraid that something terrible will happen to this child temporarily in our care that we tend to overreact. If the kid says she's sick, we never question that she isn't. If the kid says she's sick, we call a doctor—never thinking that a doctor is not necessary. We panic out of lack of confidence; we become useless in awe of a mystery we are afraid to unravel. We are paralyzed by incompetence and desperately vulnerable to smart-ass children who know how to manipulate us.

The first thing you need to do when a child tells you he is sick is to evaluate the situation for yourself. Remember, there's a very good chance that the child is not sick. Now then, if the kid comes to you with a gash on the forehead or his hand hanging off at the wrist, disregard this part—go directly to the emergency room.

How To Tell How Sick He Is

Once you have determined that the child is really sick, you must determine how sick. This often takes a few hours, so relax. There is a gray area in between announcements of illness and actual diagnosis when it could go either way: you put the child to bed, give him aspirin or Tylenol and wait and see. Soon he's either better or worse, or you are more able to judge if he's truly sick. Most childhood diseases have a short period of time in which the child's behavior is different before he actually breaks out in spots, rash, or sniffles. Never tell a child who complains of headache, stomachache, chills, or fever that he's crazy. Take him seriously, as least at the beginning, and wait and see. Especially as stepparent or part-time parent, the last thing you want to do is endanger the kid's health.

To determine how sick the child is, sleuth out these answers:

• Does he have a fever? A fever of 99° is not worth calling the doctor over. A fever of 100° probably means the child is sick. If the fever is over 100° call your doctor immediately.

• What was the state of his bowel movement? If loose, how loose? Was it mostly water? What color was it? How often does he have to move his bowels? Is there pain, cramping? Is there blood or mucus in his bowel movement?

• Check eyes, throat for redness. Check for swollen glands at throat behind ears. Are there any spots or marks inside the throat—like white dots or red sores? Do eyes burn? Are they runny?

• Check appetite. Has it changed from normal in the past twenty-four hours? Is there nausea? Vomiting? Do some foods suddenly appear to be "ucky"?

• Are there any rashes, sores, or bites out of the ordinary?

• Is your child's behavior and degree of activity normal? If he's sleepy, how much is he sleeping?

You know what your child looks, feels, and acts like normally. Any answers to those questions that are different from the norm constitute a sick child. How many positive answers will help you and the doctor determine how sick the child is. You should know the answer to these questions to help yourself determine how sick your child is and to help the doctor. He will invariably ask you these same questions.

I once kept Amy home from a day of school because she had a terrible cough and a bit of a cold. I knew she wasn't seriously ill, but I thought we'd have fun together, I was anxious to be a stay-home mommy for a day, and I was worried that she was contagious—which in itself is reason to keep your child home from school. After about two hours of game shows, breakfast in bed, and my dressing gown, she was bored out of her mind and was fast making me nuts. When the kid has too much energy for bed to contain him, he's not very sick . . . and that's as good a judge as any.

Suzy's simple questions and thoughts to determine if the kid is really sick:

• Is the kid bored? (Think, don't ask child.)

• Has he been exposed to anything in the family or at a school, camp, playgroup? (Ask if any of his friends are sick.)

• Does he have a fever? (Check by putting lips to forehead, not hand. If hot, use thermometer or fever strip.)

• Does he have swollen glands?

• When and what was the state of his last bowel movement? (Ask if he has diarrhea, usually a sign of on-coming illness.)

• How has he acted all day?

• Does he have a headache? (Ask.) Stomachache? (Ask.)

• Does he want to stay home from school?

• Does he want to go home to his real mommy?

With all children remember to consider illness as a possible manipulative ploy or emotional in origin. With stepchildren be sure to consider homesickness or anger as cause for distress.

When To Call The Doctor

There are a number of schools of thought on when to call the doctor. Since my father is a doctor, I've grown up believing that there isn't too much the doctor can do for me and am reluctant to call until I need a prescription or am in serious pain. I apply the same rule to Amy. On the other hand, in my first years as a stepmother I knew so little and felt so vulnerable when Amy's health was concerned that I called my father constantly and know that I otherwise would have called a real doctor.

This rule of thumb might help you:

• Call a doctor immediately if something drastic is wrong. A high fever, particularly if accompanied by a rash. Blood in urine or stool. Injury to the head, with even a brief loss of consciousness. Presumed broken bones.

• Call a doctor if you are so upset you need an authoritative answer to rest easy.

• Call a doctor if nothing has changed in twenty-four hours or if things are worse.

• If vomiting persists for more than twenty-four hours or is associated with severe abdominal pain.

• Should the child have a convulsion.

When you call the doctor, have the most recent temperature reading and the pharmacy's telephone number ready.

When To Call The Real Mother

There is a direct correlation between how sick your child is and how much he wants his real mother, or custodial parent. Whether he is using his illness as a means to get to his natural mother, or is genuinely sick; the last person he wants is his stepmother and the first person he wants is his real mother. In between those comes the other natural parent.

It's quite likely that the stepparent will do all the messy deeds associated with the illness and get no thanks at all, only a request to be placed with the real mother. As awful as you will feel at this moment of rejection, try to take it calmly. Remember your own mother's special bedside manner. In times of pain or panic I still want my mommy and we are all conditioned to call for her from our first days.

Only you can decide when it's time to call in the natural parent. If the custodial parent lives out of town, you're only going to call for emergencies. A phone call to the mother will have to suffice.

If the mother lives around the corner, she should be called as soon as she is requested, or maybe before she is requested if you are on speaking terms—she may be able to help with a medical history or to help you diagnose the child's ills. She will know if chicken pox has been going around the classroom while you may not.

If the child has to be hospitalized, by all means call the custodial parent.

Your feelings will be hurt, your pride will be wounded, you will be resentful and miserable. It's just another one for the joys of stepparenthood.

Telltale Signs
Of Approaching Illness

You can very often tell when your child is going to be sick before he can, or can at least recognize the warning signs—which have been mentioned as the clues in establishing illness.

• If your child's personality changes from sunny to gloomy—he could be sick.

• If your child's appetite disappears, or if he asks for strange (to him) foods—he could be sick.

• If he's sleepy, dizzy, whiny, or sluggish—he could be sick.

• If he's going to the bathroom much more often—he could be sick.

• If he doesn't "look like himself"—he could be sick.

Treat any of these symptoms with care and concern, watch for fast and further developments. Give him extra care and attention for a few hours with a wait and see attitude. Don't chastise him unless the symptoms continue without evidence of illness.

When To Go To The Emergency Room

The emergency room of any hospital is rather like a mother-in-law—you can't live without it, but you don't know how you'll survive the visit. Emergency rooms, even in the best hospitals, are usually an unhappy experience: you may have to wait for hours, there's an unbearable amount of red tape that does not concern you while your child is sick, and you may have to pay in advance. No one is particularly sympathetic and you may be forced to be exposed to worse diseases and problems than you came in with. However, when you have a child that needs immediate attention —especially when you may not have a regular pediatrician or may be in a strange city or on vacation—an emergency room visit is the best thing.

If your child is bleeding, unconscious, or obviously close to death, you will probably get taken care of right away. Otherwise, be prepared to wait. If you suspect broken bones, concussion, or animal bites, the emergency room is probably a better place than a pediatrician's office anyway because of the variety of services that can be performed instantly.

When you go to the emergency room:

• Make sure the child is warm; take along a blanket just in case.

• Be prepared to give a medical history or to be able to locate a parent who can give the child's medical history. This is essential if drugs or blood are to be administered.

• Have something for the children to play with or do, perhaps have a book to read to him while waiting.

• Determine that you will remain calm after an initial burst of hysteria to get the machinery working at the hospital.

• Have your Blue Cross, Blue Shield card with you,

know if the children are included on the policy, and a check.

• Don't lie about anything. It's not worth it.

Go to the emergency room when:

• You do not know of any other way to get quick medical aid that is obviously needed.

• A serious emergency has occurred—car accident, poisoning, fall, bruising, burning, etc.

• If your instincts tell you it's an emergency, it probably is. You could be overreacting, but it's not worth the loss of time if you're not. An emergency is different to everyone, so only life and death situations will be treated with the urgency you think your trip deserves.

How To Find A Pediatrician

• If you live in the same city as the custodial parents, use the same pediatrician even if it makes your stomach hurt. He (she) has the child's medical history and knows him. The child also knows the doctor.

• If you live in the same city you grew up in, consult your own pediatrician. If he is not still in practice, find out who he recommends or who took over his practice.

• If you don't know a doctor at all, get recommendations from women with children the same age as yours. All obstetrician/gynecologists are connected to pediatricians because they must refer their patients on delivery. Ask your obstetrician/gynecologist for some suggestions.

• Your doctor will have a list of all doctors in each speciality with their credentials printed after their names. He can find you a doctor in any city in the country through his book. He will either choose a doctor who went to his college, a doctor he did a residency with, someone he knows, or someone who has terrific-looking credentials. That may not give you a doctor you will like, but it will give you a good doctor.

• Call any local hospital and ask for recommendations by department. In pediatrics, give your requirements: "Hello, could you please recommend a black woman pediatrician who speaks Dutch and is associated with your hospital?"

• Local Medical Society.

What To Keep In The Medicine Cabinet

- Syrup of ipecac (for poisoning)
- Children's aspirin
- Lemon drops or cough drops
- Anti-itch cream or calamine lotion
- Kaopectate
- Band-Aids,Ace bandage, gauze pads, etc.
- A & D ointment
- Antiseptic, bacitracin
- Thermometer or fever strip (or both)
- Rubbing alcohol
- Heating pad
- Noxema or baby lotion
- Desenex
- Sunscreen or zinc oxide
- Vaseline
- Tylenol (acetaminophen) syrup

Giving A Child's Medical History

You will be asked for a child's medical history in the emergency room of any hospital or at any doctor's office you have never been to before. Since the child's health is at stake, make your position clear to the doctor:

• Make your relationship clear. Even if the child calls you mommy or daddy, or if the child is adopted, make sure the doctor knows you are not blood relatives.

• Don't guess on anything. If you don't know, say so. Honesty is nothing to be embarrassed about. Things can get a lot worse if you guess wrong.

• You will be asked for a history of the child's illnesses, surgery, accidents, and immunizations; possibly you will be asked the child's blood type. You may be asked if he is allergic to any drugs.

• If the procedure to be performed is routine, it won't matter that you don't know all the answers, as long as you can supply them later. If it is an emergency, locate the custodial parent immediately. The child could be allergic to penicillin and you don't know it.

Common Childhood Illnesses

Pink eye (Conjunctivitis). Conjunctivitis is a bacterial or viral infection causing the eyes to turn red, water, and burn. It's highly contagious and will sweep through play groups and classrooms like an epidemic. Isolate the infected children from the family—separate towels, linens, etc.—and discourage them from rubbing their eyes. Your doctor will prescribe an eye drop or ointment.

Diarrhea. Diarrhea may be a symptom of another problem or the result of emotions or diet. Consult your doctor after twenty-four hours, or if serious pain, blood, or mucus is associated with diarrhea. Child should drink carbonated liquids and eat light foods—nothing fried or spicy. Watch for symptoms of other diseases.

Impetigo. A skin infection as contagious as pinkeye. Child will break out in circular sores with yellow crusts, along face, arms, legs, hands, and rear end. Your doctor will prescribe an antibacterial cream or oral preparation. Isolate children just as with pinkeye.

Chicken Pox. Look for changed behavior before an eruption of tiny red blisters—usually appearing on the stomach first. Very itchy and uncomfortable. Fever common for first three to four days. Your doctor will treat with aspirin and calamine lotion. No vaccination is currently available. The first inkling of chicken pox is usually a tiny water blister on the abdomen with spreading of new crops of blisters which become raised, crusted sores over a three to five-day period.

Measles. Rash is preceded by three to four days of increasing fever, runny nose, and cough. Differs from chicken pox in that the rash is blotchy rather than individual sores. Begins on face and neck first. Bright light may be uncomfortable, but no proven harm. Your doctor will treat with aspirin or antibiotics. Vaccination available.

Mumps. You can get mumps on one side or both. Child will have dry mouth and pain in jaw, loss of appetite, and low fever. Not contagious to other family members who have already had the disease. Vaccination is available.

Rubella. ("Three-day" or "German" Measles). Fine red rash beginning behind ears and spreading to rest of body. Mild fever, rarely over 101°.

Scarlet Fever. Really just a strep throat with a rash. Onset with a high fever, vomiting, headache, sore throat, and bright red rash starting on abdomen and sparing face.

Responds beautifully to penicillin or other antibiotics if child is allergic to penicillin. Vaccination not available.

Roseola. Usually in children three months to three years. Begins with only a high fever which persists for two to three days. When fever drops to normal, child develops a rash, usually on the chest. No specific treatment. No vaccination.

8.
Thirty Days of Parenthood

I suppose my own childhood had a thread of organization to it: Saturdays, mother gave me a dollar—which was a lot of money when I was ten—and let me go to Buckhead with Marcia Rothschild, my then best friend. We walked around the stores, bought chocolate taffy, stole a Tangee lipstick or two, and saw a movie for twenty-five cents. Marcia Rothschild was older than I, so she was deemed responsible. My mother drove, her mother picked up. Saturday nights my parents always went out. I watched mother get dressed and wondered if I would ever be so grown-up. The baby-sitter always let us stay up as late as we wanted so I didn't have to read my Landmark biography under the covers with a flashlight. It was a big night indeed. Sundays we went to Sunday School and returned to find the contents of our drawers dumped on our beds—the idea being that until we cleaned up we couldn't go to bed. I always hated Sundays.

It never appeared that mother spent hours agonizing over what to do with the children. It all seemed so very easy until I became a mother. When I became a mother, I tried my mother's approach—or what I thought was my mother's approach—of letting it all just fall into place. It never did. There was no Marcia Rothschild. There was no way in the world Amy could be left alone to do anything—especially in Manhattan. And furthermore, she had no drawers of her own for me to dump out and ruin her Sunday. And she didn't even know what Sunday School was. (In fact, she didn't even know what religion she was.) As the days and weekends turned into years of experience, I found that nothing worked without careful planning. And the best success I ever had with her is when the day was organized from the beginning—as if it were a battle plan. We went from one activity to the next with such aplomb that I suddenly realized the way to make it look easy was really very hard.

Stepparents and part-time parents, much more than natural parents, feel an obligation to be with their children on their custodial days. Whereas my mother might have been delighted to shove me off on Marcia Rothschild, send my sister to art class, and my brother to Little League, my husband and I would have nothing to do with outside activities. We saw too little of Amy to share her.

So what's a parent to do? Work it out the best way he can, of course. But having exhausted the local zoo, museum of art and history, fire station, and playground, you might want to try some of the things I've used with Amy. Some of these things we have done as a family. Most of them Amy and I did in my attempts to keep her occupied, educated, and away from television.

As the years passed and my resentments grew, I turned more and more to television for my own freedom. I happened to inherit a child who couldn't read very well, had little artistic talent, and loved to watch television—a habit fostered by her natural mother. My crusade to stimulate a bright but boring child cost money, time, and patience. I found that the only projects worth doing are the ones you really care to do. If you're gritting your teeth and hating it, you'll do better to dump the kids in front of the TV. You won't be the first, or last, parent to have found your freedom through electronics.

If you choose the heroic road of enlightenment and love, remember to plan each day carefully. Have the materials you'll need and make sure everything is in working order. Remember that a child's attention span is much shorter than yours—a three-year-old child has only about a ten minute range. Even a grown-up ten-year-old cannot put in the care you can. Look at your proposed project from a child's eyes and a child's needs. Is the kitchen cabinet too high? Are the scissors a tool the child has not yet mastered? Does the project mean nothing to a four-year-old?

Always plan too much to do. You don't have to do everything on the schedule—this isn't a race—and then you'll have some preparations already done for another day. At the end of each activity—maybe even in the middle—be ready to reevaluate the plans for a possible shift in scheduling. If things are dragging along you may want to speed them up—you may need the grand finale by noon. Try to alternate activity periods with quiet times. If there are other children, by all means take advantage of them. If outdoor play is possible, include it in your lineup. Depending on the age of your children, you will either feel that you are running a small nursery school or a junior home economics class. I've always tried to do very adult things with Amy that had purpose in the real world—but she has always

been old enough to appreciate real projects. There is no reason to try to teach a four-year-old anything serious about
the art of flower arranging. Your projects should make
sense but not be too ambitious. You should care, but not
care too much. If you are more concerned with getting the
project done to perfection than having fun—or giving the
child a good time—you will be a very frustrated parent.
Also, don't forget that you can always do it better than they
can. Don't try to intimidate them with your talents. It's very
difficult to not overwhelm the kids with your own abilities
and yet get them to appreciate what it is you are teaching
them. Chances are they won't appreciate it. Think nothing
of it.

If the kids are returning from school to your home,
don't forget an after-school project. And if you work, make
sure there's something for them to do in the house—besides
get in trouble. (And watch TV.) Think of the day as a total
and add to it a full variety of experiences; something that
hasn't already been done in school is perfect for after
school.

For all projects with children, remember:

• Start off with the explanation of the project. Include a "sell." Make it exciting. Give it some meaning. Tell
the kids what is involved, what each one's job is, what can
be accomplished, and what the final product will be. If they
don't understand what they're working for, they won't enjoy the project very much.

• Assign the tasks on an age-appropriate basis. If the
child can't accomplish his part, or doesn't even understand
the project or the trip, he'll be frustrated and bored and
everyone will be miserable. Assign tasks carefully and give
plenty of encouragement and praise.

• Don't just give directions and think it's going to
take off. Pitch in. If you don't get involved, the project will

never sustain itself to the end. It's always more fun with mommy.

• Don't let the children be unsupervised—especially if danger or disaster lurk.

• Relax and have fun. Your attitude will create the mood.

DAY ONE: The Family Puppet Show

Morning: Read the children a story (or have them make one up), in which there are the same number of parts as there are children. If there are several small parts, they can be doubled up. Discuss the story, who wants to play which part (you may have to draw for the parts to be more democratic), and plan your puppet show.

Afternoon: Make puppets for each character. Depending on the age and artistic ability of the children, you can decide on the types of puppets you want to make. Here are some simple varieties:

Paper Plate Puppets. Draw the face on the back of the paper plate, garnish with yarn hair, buttons, sequins, fabric streamers, or whatever. Cut out eyes and nose (adults had better do this with young children) if they are to be worn as masks or attach plate to a paint stirring stick, a broom handle, or a yardstick.

Washcloth Puppets. Sew two washcloths together, add Styrofoam puppet head created by the children.

Paper Bag Puppets. Make out of lunch-sized brown paper bags.

Potato Puppets. Attach a baking potato to a popsicle stick—decorate as character.

Perform your family puppet show after the dinner dishes have been cleaned up.

DAY TWO: Go Fly a Kite

Morning: Sure you can go buy a kite, but it's a lot more fun to make one.

Supplies: Soft pine, bamboo, or spruce strips 1/16 of an inch thick, glue, string, brown paper bags, poster paints, crepe paper, fabric, pinking shears (optional).

The easiest kind of kite to make is the traditional diamond-shaped one. Make sure the wood is not too thick and that you bind or glue the corners, don't nail. The paper face should be glued to the frame. The tail can be decorated in any manner the child likes. You may suggest a portrait kite or a pet kite for the younger children.

Afternoon: Take a picnic lunch and go fly a kite. The excitement and outdoors will wear out anyone in an hour or two. Don't worry if the kite doesn't fly—it's a great decoration.

DAY THREE: How Green Is My Garden

Morning: Depending on the weather and the time of year, choose your gardening project appropriately. In spring you can plant seeds; in winter you can plant bulbs (indoors in pebbles).

Afternoon: Go on a nature hike looking for the kind of flowers you have just planted (or reverse the order and plant the kind of flowers you have just seen). Return home and draw pictures, press flowers, or make arrangements with the day's findings.

To Press Flowers: Flatten flower into the pages of a thick book; the telephone book is usually great. Thick flowers like roses won't press well because you can't get them flat. The flowers will press and dry in about ten days and can then be used in another project.

To Make Flower Windows: With an adult's help, iron the pressed flowers between two window-sized sheets of waxed paper. This won't preserve the flowers forever, but they'll be pretty for a few weeks.

Arrangements: Provide the kids with a cube of Styrofoam, a container (basket or bowl) for the arrangement, and then explain the fundamentals of balance and design. Show them how to place the longer-stemmed flowers in the center and surround them with shorter-stemmed ones. Even if you don't consider yourself expert at flower arranging, you probably know more than the kids, and can teach some fundamental points about balance.

DAY FOUR: The Name Game

Morning: Every child's favorite word is his name. The introduction to the name game day can begin with talking about each child's name: who he was named for, what his name means, and depending on each of the children, the sociology of names. Christopher Anderson wrote a wonderful book called The Name Game (Simon & Schuster) which will give you a lot of valuable information about names that will fascinate the children. Names that have meanings and roots are interesting to children when they are about five or six. But basic name interest begins at age three.

After the lesson, take the kids to an arts and crafts store or a hardware store where individual letters of the alphabet are sold. Choose from press-on, wooden, metal, and plastic letters of the alphabet. Let each child pick out the letters of his name (you may have to help the younger ones), teaching them the letters if need be. Also buy a plaque of wood sized according to the size of the letters and the length of the name.

Afternoon: Set up your arts and crafts table to make door plaques. If the letters are wood, they can be painted. This may take hours, so buy wooden letters. Paint or stain the plaque separately. When both are dry, nail or glue the letters on to the plaque. Hang on the child's door.

While you're helping the kids make their plaques, you can make your own that says DO NOT DISTURB.

DAY FIVE: A Musical Adventure

Morning: Take the morning to make pie pan shakers. Use large or small tin foil pie pans, two per shaker, some unpopped popcorn (pebbles will do fine), and a popsicle stick, plastic knife, spoon, or fork, or tongue depressor. Staple the tins together with the popcorn inside and the popsicle stick as the handle. Each child will need two shakers. The tins can be decorated with fabric, buttons, shells, or crepe paper streamers if desired.

Afternoon: Teach the children about rhythm. Play a fast, peppy song they like over and over again on your record player. Teach them to listen for the rhythm track. Then get them to participate along with the record, shaking their instruments along with the rhythm section of the song. A performance for the family after dinner should be considered.

WARNING: Younger children will be able to enjoy making the shakers and using them, but will not be able to hear the rhythm track or be able to keep time. After about age six, the refinements of sound can be better heard and understood.

DAY SIX: Stained Glass Study

Morning: If the children are old enough to appreciate art and learn anything about it, take them on a morning tour of the local institutions using stained glass. Make sure you have your itinerary planned in advance, don't wander aimlessly. Try churches, synagogues, old houses, and antique stores. Then go home and make your own stained glass.

Afternoon: If your children are too young to understand the art of stained glass, skip the tour and the lecture and jump right into this project. (It's basically a half-day project, so you'll need something for the other half.)

Supplies: Colored and clear baking crystals obtained from your local crafts or hobby shop (primary colors and clear are sufficient in range; you don't have to buy a package of every color), metal cookie cutters, string or metal loops or paper clips or Christmas tree loops.

Directions: On a metal cookie sheet (cover first with tin foil) place the metal cookie cutters and fill about one quarter of an inch deep with the crystals. Make sure the crystals are inside the cookie cutter, not outside. Don't let the children eat the crystals. Bake in 400° oven for 10-15 minutes until the crystals melt and fuse. Remove cookie cutter immediately (adults do this with pot holder) and let creation dry. You will then have a stained glass-looking ornament for Christmas tree or mobile making.

Or, make a paperweight or medallion mobile. Remember those flowers you pressed and dried previously? Melt a layer of clear crystals, then place the dried flower inside the medallion, cover with more crystals, and bake. You'll have a perfectly preserved dried flower in a paperweight or medallion form. You can use this same method with shells, coins, or small, flat treasures.

DAY SEVEN: Just Like Me

This can be an all-day project. Help your children make soft sculptures of themselves.

Supplies: Brown paper (wrapping or Kraft paper which is sold by the roll in any dime store—or you can steal a piece from your office's mail room; don't fold it, roll it when you bring it home, crayons, poster paints, yarn, fabric bits, marking pens, stapler, batting.

Have the child lie down on a flat surface over a double length of brown paper. An older child or adult will then trace completely around the child, staying as close to the body as possible. Make sure arms are positioned completely within the brown paper. Cut out the two figures and complete the portrait. One side should be the child's front, the other side his back. The children may want to consult mirrors. Add yarn for hair, if desired.

When both sides are completed, fill with batting and staple all the way around. (This makes a great gift.) If you only see your child once a year, you may want to collect the sculptures as proof of his growth.

DAY EIGHT: Basket Painting

Morning: This is a half-day project which can be combined with flower arranging or gift giving, or a field trip to a hospital with a get well basket for the sick children or needy.

Supplies: Any number of cheap baskets, with or without handles, depending on their end purpose. Glossy paint (there's a brand called Wet Paint that is perfect—it's ninety-nine cents for a jar and comes in lots of great colors), acrylics, paintbrushes, varnish.

Paint the basket, one side at a time, letting it dry fully before attempting the next side. Supervise carefully.

It even helps if you show a sample beforehand so the kids can understand what they are doing. (They are not painting a picture on a basket but painting a complete basket and they should understand the difference.) The paint job should completely cover the straw. Only when all sides are dry do you decorate the painted basket. Using contrasting colors of paint, paint any design desired. Stripes and squiggles work just as well as polka dots and flowers. Discourage scene painting and slogans. Don't forget to have the artist sign and date the underside of the basket. When the design is totally dry, varnish for protection.

Afternoon: Spend the afternoon or the drying time periods making something to go in the basket. Even if you clean out your shelves to donate unused canned goods to the poor, it gives the children a great project.

DAY NINE: It's The Berries

This can be a half-day or whole-day project, depending on the time of year, availability of the ingredients, and age of your children. It does coordinate nicely with the basket-painting project because it can provide jam in jars to put in the baskets.

Morning: Gather ye berries while ye may. If the children can pick their own berries, it will greatly enhance their interest in this project. Even if you live in the city, within an hour's drive there may be a place you can take them for berry picking (in season). Many farming areas actually have places where you can pay a fee and go pick the fruits for a day or half-day.

If the berries are not available on the tree or bush, get them at a grocery store. If this is a winter project, use dried or frozen berries. You can freeze some of your fresh pick for winter and remind the kids of the day they picked the fruit.

Then:

1. Clean and hull the fruit. Make sure you have enough for snitching. You can expect the children to eat while they cook. Supervise this carefully, or you may have cherry pits where you least expect them. Crush or cut up fruit as recipe states.

2. Follow a recipe in any cookbook for a jam, jelly,

or preserve. Different fruits require different ingredients, so don't transpose a recipe unless you're sure it will work.

3. Jam making is easy but tedious, so it's the perfect project for children. But you must supervise. Let them stir, teach them how to pour paraffin, and advise on the importance of sterilized jam jars. But beware of the dangers with paraffin and cooking.

Once a child has made his own jam, he'll probably never want store bought again. Make sure you make enough to take home to custodial parents or to give as gifts. And have lots of peanut butter on hand.

Afternoon: If you are still looking for a project to round out your berry picking day, have the children make labels for the jam jars. Any office supply store or dime store will have plain white (some have colored) labels with sticky backs. Crayons and magic markers can make personal labels with maker's name, the name of the jam, and the date. Remember that children can't write small letters so they may not get too much information on the label. Show them some other labels or give them ideas of how to decorate them. (A picture of the berry in full color makes a perfect label.)

DAY TEN: A Jewelry Project

Morning: This is a half-day project unless it is combined with another half-day of source hunting for the jewelry. Children three and up can make rudimentary jewelry. After age six there's some interest in making real jewelry. Make sure you plan this project to match your child's abilities and interests. If you are combining two different-aged children in the same project, make sure the younger doesn't eat the materials of the older. Beads for toddlers should be too big to swallow and strung without needles. There are bead kits on the market, or you can make your own.

Here are some ideas:

● Make beads out of empty spools of thread. Paint them or cover with bits of fabric or tissue paper.

● Make beads in a pottery class.

● Search shops and outdoors for shells with holes, pretty rocks, or appropriate treasures for jewelry making.

Other Supplies: Cord or leather thong, yarn or wire for stringing. Macaroni, paper clips, dried bread dough, or papier-mâché, and buttons make stringable ornaments.

A hobby store or a fabric store will have a wide selection of cords. My local fabric store has "silk" cord for nineteen cents a yard.

Play dress-up with the newly made jewelry.

DAY ELEVEN: Clorox Painting

This is a half-day project for morning or afternoon. It takes a lot of supervision.

Supplies: Solid-colored T-shirt, sheet, or wall hanging with enough color in it for the Clorox design to show up. Dark, bright colors are best. (If such an item doesn't exist, dye a white one.) Make sure your kids don't eat the dye (or drink the Clorox). A thin-tipped paintbrush or, better yet, an artist's pen (not a rapidograph). (Tips for the pen cost under ten cents.) Some Clorox in a dish.

To get a clear Clorox painting, design, or name, the artist must go very slowly, making even strokes against the fabric. Mistakes can only be corrected with redyeing. The object is to put the Clorox where you want the design to show up—it will eat away the color and leave your design in white.

After the design has come up sufficiently, rinse the fabric to get the Clorox out or it will eat a hole in the fabric. Let dry and voilà—a personalized project.

Amy and I have had our best success with names and simple messages rather than pictures.

T-shirt design has become a new industry, so you can modify this project into any number of variations. You can iron on T-shirt designs, have the youngsters sew on button borders, make ribbons pictures, or paint right on the shirts with fabric paints or crayons. You can stud clothes, write names in glitter, and do just about anything.

DAY TWELVE: Card Making

Make cards and envelopes out of construction paper and then decorate them. This is a particularly nice project near Christmas or Valentine's Day, but also makes a good gift or helps make thank-you note writing more bearable when the child can write on personally created notepaper.

All craft shops sell ready-made blank cards and envelopes (Strathmore makes a package of twenty cards and envelopes of high quality paper for four dollars.) It's more fun to use the Strathmore because it doesn't appear home-made and impresses the children that they are making a serious piece of artwork.

Cards can be decorated by many methods; here are a few suggestions:

Potato Printing. Cut a potato in half. Carve in a design or name. Apply thick tempera paint and stamp the card. You can do the same thing with a fruit or vegetable with a natural design in it if the child is too young to carve his own artwork.

Rubber Stamps. Buy them at an office supply store, crafts shop, or have them custom-made with words or designs. With the stamps get the ink pads which come in a lot of colors. Perhaps you want to buy the whole alphabet so the kids can set up a print shop.

Silk Screen. Get the supplies in your local craft shop. Only older children should silk-screen as it is involved and messy. If you do teach them to silk-screen, remember that you can make more than cards.

Stencils. The kids can cut stencils and paint them or you can cut and they can fill in. You can also stencil more than cards. (Furniture, floors, and walls look great when stenciled.)

DAY THIRTEEN: Fabric Techniques

This is a better half-day than full-day project but can be spread out or broken into two different projects for different days.

Morning: Batik T-shirts or wall hangings. Batik is an ancient method of artwork in which a design is drawn in wax and dyed with the wax then melted out. The results are similar to Clorox painting but allow for much more finesse. Although you can buy batik kits, all you really need is the special wax and dye, usually less than a dollar a color. You can batik sheets and pillow cases, lengths of fabric for wall hangings or stitched goods, or T-shirts. Best for children over seven.

Afternoon: Tie-dyeing can be done by much younger children and while it's no longer a fashion rage, it's still a lot of fun. Even a three-year-old, with help and supervision, can be a successful tie-dyer. Rit Dye Company makes a free brochure, which you don't need for elementary dyeing. The idea in tie-dyeing is that the fabric will not absorb the dye wherever it is tied, be it tied in knots or tied with string. Let the kids tie strings around a garment, then dip in Rit dye. Untie. Instant design. Let dry.

DAY FOURTEEN: Refinish A Piece Of Furniture

This is easily an all-day project and could be stretched out longer. Start with an old piece of wooden furniture—one you have in the house or purchase at a junk shop, flea market, or Salvation Army store. It should not be a huge piece of furniture and if you expect active help from the children, should be for someone they care about. The furniture must be stripped, sanded, painted, stained, or varnished and can then be stenciled. Each of these steps takes a lot of elbow grease and can use the helpful hands of children who are old enough to know not to drink the shellac.

DAY FIFTEEN: Pillowcase Costumes

Morning: Choose a historic theme and help the children to costume themselves with the use of pillowcases. Let the kids cut neck and arm holes in a single pillow case and don their costume. Costumes can be decorated with yarn, painted with poster paint, dyed with Rit, or stitched. You can usually start teaching eight-year-olds how to sew on the sewing machine. Pillowcases aren't really cheap, but they do last, so these costumes can be used over and over.

Afternoon: Stage a play wearing the costumes or provide the props for a fantasy time related to the period of the costumes.

DAY SIXTEEN: Collage and Decoupage

These are two different techniques that are rather similar and make a good all-day activity or you can use each as a half-day project.

Morning: Make a collage to be framed, collecting a variety of treasures of a rather flat nature in different textures. Combine photographs with fabric and ribbons and wallpaper and a few old buttons. Anything pretty that works together. Have a theme or general picture for the collage. I always use a vase full of flowers on a table because it takes no artistic talent whatsoever.

Supplies: Canvas large enough for you to work on (at least eleven-by-fourteen inches), glue, leftover pretties you have been saving.

Cover the canvas with a background—I usually use half tin foil and half wallpaper. Add the foreground—a piece of fabric for the tablecloth in this case. Then make the vase and add flowers—I use paper cutout flowers with some dried flowers. Balance the picture to your eye's content. Amy filled in the tin foil part with the strips of old ribbon and a lace doily with her picture on it. Have the artist sign and date. Frame. Amy's collage, which was a Christmas gift to her mother, cost about ten dollars to make (including frame) and could well hang in an art gallery. Though she isn't even very artistic, the proper hodgepodge created a beautiful piece.

Afternoon: Decoupage is easier than collage and is good for younger children who will not understand the artistic balance necessary for a collage. Simply cover a board—or better, a household item (I suggest a tin lunch box)—with pictures cut out of magazines or books. Glue down, shellac when finished. It takes no talent whatsoever. Youngsters love to rip pages out of magazines. Try to stick to a theme—all pictures of pets or flowers, for a bit of artistic measure. Older children can save things from a vacation or a summer spent with you and then put the collection into a decoupage. Art stores sell little boxes and plaques especially made for decoupage projects.

DAY SEVENTEEN: Plaster of Paris Molds and Castles In The Air

Morning: Plaster of paris molds only interest young children and once made are seldom exciting. You can possibly entice an older child to get interested in molds by explaining that a collection of molds over the years shows how much the child has grown.

Buy plaster of paris in an art or hobby store, mix with water, and shape into hand-sized balls. Squish to medallion size with the palm, sculpt into shape, and then press the old hand right into the plaster for a minute or two.

Let it dry overnight. Painting and shellacking the molds on another day will be another half-day project.

For older children you can get more excitement by making gifts or bookends from plaster of paris molds.

Afternoon: Another half-day project, this one for children of all ages. Go to your local grocery store, or call a moving company and invest in a large-sized cardboard box or two. Have the children paint it with poster paint to the fantasy home of their choosing—a fortress, a castle, a cave, or an automobile. They can spend the rest of the afternoon playing in their creation and leave you free to relax. This coordinates well with the pillowcase costume project.

DAY EIGHTEEN: Cooking

Cooking can be an all-day or half-day affair, depending on the project and the age of your children. I've found that half days are better because a lot of control has to be used while cooking and it's too much to ask children to be controlled all day long. Although there are numerous dummy kiddie recipes, I have had best results in making grown-up dishes of some difficulty. For Chinese food I find Amy far more efficient than a Cuisinart—and cheaper. Pasta making takes a great deal of time and is terribly exciting because it's much like a miracle—you start with eggs and flour and end up with noodles and then dinner. Ditto for pizza and dinner or dessert crepes. Being able to eat something they have personally created is exciting for children —especially if they are fixing something exotic.

You can go for a whole day if you have a bread-baking marathon. Be sure each child has a book or some other activity for the time period while the dough is rising—and don't let them peek too many times. Make more than one kind of bread—for the freezer and for gifts— to keep the kids busy. Bread making takes a lot of time and is usually very satisfying.

DAY NINETEEN: Ceramics

This is a good controlled half-day project to be mixed with an active project. I used to spend morning with Amy at the pottery shop, take her to lunch, and then go to the beach where I read a book and she ran around and went swimming. Even at nine years of age she didn't have the control to go all day in the pottery shop—I might not have either.

There are two types of ceramics work you and your children can do—check the yellow pages of your local phone book for locations. There's green ware—already sculpted pieces waiting to be decorated and fired, and clay, which means starting from scratch. Younger children can make pinch pots and cups. It takes a lot of strength to use the wheel. Amy—who is strong and big for her age—had trouble when she was nine. I still find it a struggle.

You can make beads, Christmas ornaments, mobiles, and coffee mugs without any training or ability whatsoever. And it's terribly rewarding.

DAY TWENTY: The Butcher, The Baker, The Candlestick Maker

Morning: Give a little lesson on candles and candle-making before you start this project. You may even want to take a field trip to a nearby candle store where children over the age of four will be fascinated by the various colors, shapes, and smells.

You can make your own candles easily but with constant adult supervision, as hot paraffin or wax can be very dangerous. Paraffin is also highly flammable, so make sure you melt it in a water bath rather than directly on the stove.

Supplies: Juice cans, soup cans, milk cartons, or any other peel-away shapes. String for wick (hobby shops sell wicks which are already weighted) with paper clip on the end. Food coloring, paraffin, scent (optional).

You can attach the string to a pencil and pour around it, or have a child hold the string—which will be cut down to a normal wick size only *after* the candle has cooled. Don't have too short a wick or you'll have trouble. Let candles fully harden before peeling away the container. You can probably get the children to help you make a special candlelight dinner to use their creations.

Check with your hobby store if you want to get into more elaborate candle styles.

Afternoon: Soap making is much like candle making, so you may want to combine them in one project...but you don't get the soapy results for several months, so you will lose some gratification unless you combine with another project.

Supplies: Lard or a can of bacon grease, salt, ammonia, sugar, scent.

Melt down the lard, combine with salt, ammonia,

sugar, and scent, stir and pour into either cardboard boxes lined with wax paper or milk cartons. Set aside for three months to cure. After one month, score the soap, which will now be partially hardened, so it will be easier to cut into cakes. Don't be alarmed if the soap turns color over the three-month period.

___

DAY TWENTY-ONE: Festival Of The Masks

Morning: Cut out and color paper masks for fantasy play or a family drama project. There are a number of different ways to make masks but I found a delightful book for Amy that I recommend: Michael Grater's *Cut And Color Paper Masks,* a Dover Coloring Book ($1.50) with nine different masks already drawn. All you have to do is color, cut out, and assemble.

You can tie the masks on with yarn, string, or better yet, elastic string bought at your dime store or fabric store.

You can also make masks from paper bags, paper plates, and egg cartons.

Afternoon: Combine the masks with fantasy play— either a drama, a history lesson, or coupled with a homemade castle or play prop.

___

DAY TWENTY-TWO: Quilting

You can make this an all day affair if you don't mind children dropping in and out, and have plenty of food and good music. Host a real live quilting bee with a lot of friends and their children or start small on a project the children can handle themselves—like quilting pot holders. Bring out your fabric remnant bag and cut squares to be patched together into one piece of fabric the size of a pot holder (nine-by-nine inches). Seam three sides of the finished patched piece and backing, creating a pocket that you can fill with a light layer of batting. Then stitch all the layers together in straight lines (crisscross squares or diagonals) and you have a quilted pot holder.

If you choose to just do the patchwork, you can send out the quilting and not have to do it yourself. Quilting is a big job, especially for children.

You may choose to modify the project by doing appliques out of the same remnants saved up. I made the Amy sheets by appliquing her name and a field of flowers out of calico fabric and ribbons. You can do appliqued pot holders, sheets, wall hangings, or T-shirts. Several firms make kits for beginners to get the hang of quilting and appliqueing.

Children can begin stitching with a blunt needle at age three. Sewing should not be sexually biased!

Price/Stern/Sloan publishes a quilting coloring book which is a great introduction to traditional quilt patterns.

DAY TWENTY-THREE: Stencil The World

You can stencil anything with any degree of sophistication. Young children may be perfectly content learning how to stencil on paper bags or drawing paper. Older children may like to stencil their name on T-shirts. But the real excitement comes when you get the children to help you create a stencil transformation . . . by doing a floor, a piece of furniture, or the walls or ceiling. Amy and I stenciled the bathroom of our country house. It took almost all day, and is a source of constant smiles.

Morning: Choose the stencil design and cut it out. We first pored over books of folk art, stenciled walls in historic homes and old-fashioned designs before deciding on a traditional flower basket motif. We chose the design because it was clean and simple and neither of us has any tremendous amount of artistic ability. I drew the design with a pencil on a shirt cardboard, cut it out with an Exacto knife, and then we practiced on newspaper.

Afternoon: You'll make better time if you have more than one stencil and more than one child. I taped the stencil on the bathroom walls—which had just been painted white—and Amy painted in the design with terra-cotta latex paint. She used both a paintbrush and a sponge to see which technique she preferred and ended up with the sponge for smoother color. I carefully removed the stencil and applied it to other portions of the wall. By late afternoon we had an entirely different bathroom and we were both quite pleased with ourselves. Latex washes off, so we were free to get very dirty.

DAY TWENTY-FOUR: Making Books

Introduce the children to the wonderful world of books by helping them to make their own. They can cut pictures out of magazines, paste in mementos, or do original drawings to tell a story of their summer or make up an original tale. You can bind the book or staple it, making covers from shirt cardboard covered with fabric remnants or pasted in pictures. For younger children, a simple theme like pets will keep them busy most of the day. Older children should be challenged more and stimulated to write something original or to team up on a project with one child illustrating and another writing. You can also put out a family newspaper or magazine if this venture is successful.

DAY TWENTY-FIVE: Hat Tricks

Keep a collection of hats in your closet for use in role playing and character development. Get the children to assume the part of the person who wears the hat, and to interact in a real-life drama. You will be able to collect a variety of hats at garage sales and flea markets without spending a lot of money. This game doesn't need much adult supervision and is great for rainy days. You can supplement its progress by making your own hats and then acting out the parts in the afternoon.

Hats to collect:
- A tiara
- Chinese straw hat
- Old-fashioned sunbonnet
- Indian warbonnet or headdress
- Policeman's cap, fireman's hat, etc.
- Maid's lace cap, nurse's cap, etc.

DAY TWENTY-SIX: Papier Mâché

I have never had great success with papier mâché, but maybe you can do better. It's good for various building projects and can give a lot of satisfaction, especially in mask making.

Shred paper, I recommend tissue paper, but you can use newspaper or butcher paper or even paper towels, and soak in hot water until pliable. Mix with a flour and water paste until the proper consistency for molding. Mold. Let dry and paint.

DAY TWENTY-SEVEN: The Family Tree

The popularity of *Roots* has made everyone more conscious of his family history. A day can easily be spent in tracing one's family and drawing a family tree. I remember being particularly offended when a girl in my third grade class reported that she was directly related to Daniel Boone, so I've always tried to begin my family tree with Moses. You needn't go back that far to have a lot of fun. Family research is also a good way to introduce children to libraries and researching methods.

DAY TWENTY-EIGHT: Making Bookends

A great building project for children of all ages is the

construction of bookends. You'll need four pieces of wood, two inches thick, six inches long, and four inches wide. Nail two pieces together in an L-shape to form the bookends, and then decorate with decoupage or paint and shellac. A great gift. Youngsters should be encouraged to use hammer and nails starting at an early age. And there should be no sexual discrimination about building projects.

DAY TWENTY-NINE: There But For Fortune

Teach kids about tea leaves, astrology, and fortune telling with some books on the subject, then let each of them try. You can round out the day by making your own fortune cookies and writing your own messages. Fortune-telling talents will be continually called on at school carnivals and birthday parties. If your older children show a flair for this kind of thing, they might want to hire out to make a little extra money. Making costumes for their adventures will only heighten the fun. Remember: fortune tellers should never give out bad news.

DAY THIRTY: Frame Up

There are many frame-it-yourself shops opening in art and hobby stores and children will take pride in building their own frames. It's painstaking work, so it takes lots of time, and there's always someone in the shop to give the lesson, so you can sit back. Frame one of the kid's original paintings, sketches, photographs, or wall hangings. You may also want to get into frame decoration by buying an unfinished frame and staining or painting it before building the frame. Make sure young children aren't near dangerous blades in this project.

9.
Everything You Need to Know To Start a Relationship With Someone Else's Child

The material for this chapter was compiled from existing books on child development, interviews with schoolteachers and parents, and questionnaires filled out by hundreds of schoolchildren in the Southern California area. While the mix of economic, ethnic and social backgrounds was complete, the children are all from various communities in Southern California.

Because each child, and each adult for that matter, is different, there is no reason for alarm if your children, grandchildren or stepchildren do not fit into the profile for their appropriate age. As children grow older, they grow more sophisticated, although not necessarily at the same time as other children. You may have a young ten year old or an old three year old, and perhaps you should read the chapters before and after the age you are investigating for a better understanding of who and what you are dealing with.

There are many modes of behavior that are completely appropriate for a particular age, a fact that always shocks an instant parent into confusion. The uninitiated parent may be furious that an eleven year old is so sloppy, only to find out that the same child was neater at age eight and will become neater again in a few years—sloppiness is simply part of being eleven years old.

I have not provided information on children younger than two because it is unlikely that you will have to deal with children any younger. (Few men leave wives with infants in their arms to remarry immediately.) Children over the age of twelve are also excluded from the profiles merely because once they are that age there isn't too much you can do but pray.

All information in these chapters has been studied and verified by Dr. Britton.

Suggesting toys and books is particularly tricky because of the personal nature of the gift. The titles of books herein are ones that I personally love, that are either classics, best-sellers or new and popular titles. Never buy or give a book to a child unless you have read it! Likewise, with a toy make sure you know how it works, what its dangers are and if you believe in it. I have not recommended any toys that perpetrate violence or war games. Your local toy store, bookstore or library will have salespeople with whom you can consult.

TWO

General characteristics: Two-year-olds change tremendously over a one-year period so that early twos will resemble babies and older twos will be quite grown-up, some will even be able to articulate their needs. Twos need considerable supervision and care and will wear out even the most energetic of parents. May still use pacifier, have favorite "blanky" or toy, suck thumb or bite fingernails, teethe, use car seat and stroller, want to be carried some of the time. Cannot walk great distances and has a very short attention span. Will put anything in mouth. Most common age for accidents. Has separation anxiety.

Appetite: Twos eat one big meal a day and a mid-morning and afternoon snack. They like some baby food, but mostly adult food.

Bathing and grooming habits: Prefers bath to shower. Usually enjoys the bath as a playtime. Must be supervised.

Birthday festivities: Limit to a few children and their parents for a short party.

Books: Likes nursery rhymes with repetition and rhythm and tactile books with things to touch. May start identifying first letters of alphabet. Recommended books are "The Nutshell Library" books by Maurice Sendak, *The Tale of Peter Rabbit* by Beatrix Potter, *Millions of Cats* by Wanda Gag, Dr. Seuss' ABC, any of the "Frances the Badger" books by Russell Hoban.

Entertainment: Twos have a very short attention span for entertainment not of their own making. They may watch some parts of a television show, probably while playing with something else. They cannot watch a movie, puppet show or any theatrical endeavor with complete understanding or ease. They enjoy digging in sand or dirt. Exploring drawers, tasting everything within their grasp and trying all mommy's makeup are good forms of entertainment.

Favorite color: Red.

Favorite holidays: His birthday, Christmas, Valentine's Day, Easter. No interest in Halloween or Thanksgiving.

Food preferences: Meat, fruit, milk. Dislikes green vegetables. Has favorite foods and may refuse to eat anything else.

Gifts: Stories on records, toys that can be pushed or pulled, plastic tricycles, trucks, wagons, Play Doh, giant "ride 'em" gifts, Lego assembly toys.

Joke: Doesn't understand word jokes. Funny is physical—a surprise tickle, a pratfall, hide-and-seek, etc.

Motor capabilities: Can walk, but not quite erect. Goes up stairs one at a time with one lead foot. Probably cannot stand on one foot. Can run, push, pull, kick a ball, hold glass or cup, feed self with some help. Cannot use scissors, tie shoes, dress self (but is learning to undress self).

Parental preference: Mother.

Peer play: Little if any play with others. Prefers to play alone, but may enjoy playing in the company of other children.

Physical characteristics: Height—32–35 inches. Weight—20–30 pounds.

School: May be ready for day-care or nursery school.

Sexuality: Conscious of own genitals and may touch them. Interested in all bathroom activities and seeing others undressed.

Skills: Trying to make sentences to express ideas. May begin a sentence over and over again trying to find the right words. Likes to name things and repeat words. Has a vocabulary of 200–300 words. Gets terribly frustrated with inability to express himself. This frustration may lead to temper tantrums that should be ignored. Tends to say no even when he means yes. Likes to color on plain paper, finger paint, mold clay. Usually too soon to tell if real artistic talent exists. Cannot hold crayon properly. Sings phrases of songs and keeps time to the music. Cannot tell time.

Sleeping patterns: Wake-up—6:30–7:30 A.M. Bedtime—7:30–8:00 P.M. Nap—yes. Moves from crib to real bed. Likes to have book read to him. Has favorite toys to say good night to. Sleeps with blanket or stuffed animal. Calls mommy for glass of water and trip to the bathroom.

Television: Most children begin watching television before they are two and are fully aware of programs such as "Sesame Street" at age two. Not yet influenced by advertising.

Toilet training: Most twos are ready to be toilet trained, a process that will be successful only when the child is ready and not before. Let the custodial parent take the lead in toilet training. Child fears bladder-control failure.

Toys and games: Tricycle, wheelbarrow, toy trucks and cars, large beads, clay, finger paints, soap-bubble pipe, pegboard, jars with tops that screw on and off, colored baskets, nonworking telephone, large-sized crayons and plain paper, magnets, tea-party sets, blocks, dolls, teddy bear.

Trips: Short walks to see animals, flowers, nature, parks, zoos, train station. Too young to appreciate historical places, long drives, plays, movies, theater, etc.

THREE

General characteristics: Tremendous freedom comes to three-year-olds who are toilet trained and can communicate their needs. They are much more grown-up than two-year-olds. May sometimes ask to be carried or pushed in stroller or supermarket basket. Very self-reliant.

Appetite: Fair to picky.

Bathing and grooming habits: Likes to take a bath if it's entertaining (toys, bubbles, etc.). Wants to get in and out of tub without adult help. Goes through motions of washing with washcloth.

Birthday festivities: Invite just a few other children with their parents for cake and ice cream, and outdoor play. Too young for organized play or trips.

Bladder control: Threes need to be reminded to go to bathroom every two hours. May have night-time accidents.

Books: The Runaway Bunny by Margaret Wise Brown, *Bruno Munari's ABC* by Bruno Munari, *Are You My Mother?* by P. D. Eastman, any Dr. Seuss book, Dr. Doolittle books, Madeline books by Ludwig Bemelmans.

Entertainment: Three-year-olds have a short attention span and are not ready for any formal entertainment. It's unlikely that they can sit through a half-hour television show and completely understand it, but they may take delight in short puppet shows or theatrical entertainments. Some threes are introduced to the theater, ballet, and opera.

Favorite color: One of the primaries.

Favorite holidays: His birthday, Christmas, Valentine's Day, Halloween. Thanksgiving is boring.

Food preferences: Milk, fruit, meat, desserts, sweets. Beginning to accept vegetables, preferably raw. Has special favorites he will request.

Gifts: Tunnel of Fun (Creative Playthings), Playskool Village, Lego assembly toys, Muppet puppets, doll house, Create a Story (Kiddicraft), Electro (Jumbo).

Joke: Doesn't understand word jokes. Thinks pratfalls and physical humor are funny. Loves to be tickled.

Motor capabilities: Walks completely upright. Can

undo buttons. Uses spoon well, holds cup by handle and glass with one hand. May be able to ride tricycle. Dresses self. Has trouble telling front from back. Undressing still easier than dressing.

Parental preference: Mother.

Peer play: Plays independently, but in the company of older children. Prefers outdoors. May have imaginary friends. Cooperative play is just beginning.

Physical characteristics: Weight—32 pounds. Height —38 inches.

Responsibilities: Can help clear dishes, carry silverware to the table, help feed pets, hang clothes on pegs.

School: Day-care or nursery.

Sexuality: Aware of own genitalia and may masturbate. Often grabs or touches genitals as a sign of needing the bathroom. Notices the differences between men and women and will probably ask about them. Great fascination with bathroom habits of adults.

Skills: Three-year-olds develop enough skills to enable them to cross the threshold from toddlers into real people. They usually speak in full sentences and can make clear what they want to do. Precocious threes may be learning to read or are at least memorizing words in books, on doors (men and women), or on labels. The three-year-old may very well have memorized a storybook and will know if you change the words or skip something. He loves to tear things out of magazines, but cannot master a scissors with much dexterity. He likes to think he can dress himself, but can do only the simplest dressing (he probably can't put on an overcoat). Learning to do buttons and use zippers. Can master Velcro closing easily and is proud to be able to do so. Cannot buckle shoes. Rides small bikelike toys, but not a real bicycle. Uses potty seat. Can memorize words to songs, even whole songs, and likes to clap hands and sing or dance along to music. Spontaneous dancing to music is common. Likes to build sand castles, dirt tunnels, build with blocks. Artistic talent begins to emerge—likes to paint with water colors and mold clay.

Sleeping patterns: Wake-up—7:00–7:30 A.M. Bedtime—7:30–8:00 P.M. Nap—maybe. Sleeps in real bed.

Television: Television viewing habits are formed at this age. Parents who allow three-year-olds to watch a lot of television are setting a pattern that will carry through their entire childhood. While kids can get hooked after age three, this is a very vulnerable age in developing independence. Therefore, the child should be encouraged to develop himself as a person rather than waste his time in front of the TV set. While vocabulary is growing rapidly at this age, it will be hindered greatly if the child only watches television. Child prefers Saturday morning cartoons and animated specials. Likes "Sesame Street." Thinks advertisements are part of the show.

Toys and games: Blocks, tricycle, dress-up collection, finger paints, wagons, simple art supplies, xylophone, play telephone.

Trips: Three-year-olds are getting old enough for outings, field trips, and simple vacations. They tire easily and cannot be expected to pay too much attention, but they enjoy seeing and touching animals, splashing in water (many threes can swim), and playing with other children in outdoor activities. Too young to enjoy fishing trips, sightseeing, museums, or historical sights.

FOUR

General characteristics: Bursting ahead in a boastful manner, a four likes to brag and boss others around. Likes to show-off and perform. Tall tales are common. Overdramatic. Name-calling and tattling are common. Imitates adults. A four will probably dawdle a lot because he has no understanding of time. Wants anything he makes to be admired and displayed. Big age for how-and-why questions. His favorite topic is himself.

Appetite: Getting better. Demands favorite foods.

Bathing and grooming habits: Able to wash self but must be supervised in bathroom. Prefers tub to shower. Likes toys in bath. May dawdle. Can dry self fairly well.

Birthday festivities: Several friends—both sexes—for games like "pin the tail on the donkey," "drop the clothespin in the bottle," and "pass the bean bag." Hats, blowers, and all the goings-on of a traditional party. Each child present should receive a favor to take home.

Bladder control: Fully toilet trained. Needs to be reminded to go to the bathroom at three-hour intervals and before leaving house. May get up during night to urinate. Rarely wets bed.

Books: Cat In The Hat Dictionary by Dr. Seuss, Richard Scarry books, _The Enormous Crocodile_ by Roald Dahl, _The Messy Rabbit_ by Ruth Nivola.

Entertainment: Fours are beginning to get the hang of entertainment as an art form. They want to watch television, go to the movies, be taken with grown-ups to the theater, ballet, or concerts (especially children's concerts). They will probably get bored, wriggle around, or fall asleep, but they want to go.

Favorite color: Blue for boys. Pink for girls.

Favorite holidays: Birthday, Christmas, Halloween, Valentine's Day.

Food preference: Hamburgers, chocolate ice cream, snacks, juice and cookies, fruit.

Gifts: Who Lives Here? (Victory), Micronauts, Lego

toys, Candyland board game, Mattel typewriter, painting easel.

Joke: What's got wheels and flies? A garbage truck.

Motor capabilities: Can talk and eat at the same time, throw a ball overhand, cut on a line with scissors, tie and lace shoes, stand on one foot, dress self slowly (knows front from back), comb hair, brush teeth, ride tricycle, skip (but not hop). Cannot jump rope.

Parental preference: Mommy.

Peer play: Enjoys the company of others, not too picky about sex of friend. Prefers group play or several single partners, not one best friend. Enjoys company of the neighborhood children.

Physical characteristics: Weight—36 pounds. Height —41 inches.

Responsibilities: Fours can help with pet care, but cannot be totally responsible for animals. Because they still don't know right from wrong they cannot take too heavy a responsibility. Can carry things to the table, hang clothes on pegs, clean bathtub ring, put clothes in laundry hamper, help make bed, put away toys. This is an important age for learning to do chores that child will be able to do better next year.

School: Fours are definitely old enough for some type of preschool education or formal playgroup. They enjoy being with peers and having a full or partial day's activities out of the house like older children.

Sexuality: "I'll show you mine, if you show me yours." May want to know where babies come from. Boys may hold genitals and may masturbate.

Skills: Can probably count to ten and say alphabet, memorize books, frequently can read by memorization.

Sleeping patterns: Wake-up—7:00–7:30 A.M. Bedtime—7:00–7:30 P.M. Naps—probably. May be afraid of the dark and ask for a night light.

Television: Loves television and advertisements. Can't concentrate on entire program. "The Muppets," "Sesame Street," and cartoons are favorites. Making the transition to more grown-up programming, the child has even more opportunity to get "hooked." Besides cartoons and animated shows, a four-year-old can easily follow adventure stories. Old reruns of "Davy Crockett" and "Jim Bowie" are favorites, as are old sit-coms like "Bewitched," "I Dream of Jeannie," and "I Love Lucy." Most police, private-eye, and love stories do not interest the four-year-old—yet. May be highly influenced by what he sees on television and become afraid of a character or situation seen on TV. Nightmares inspired by TV shows are not uncommon. Highly susceptible to advertising during TV shows and will ask for whatever is advertised—be it food or toys.

Toys and games: Four-year-olds want all the toys and games they see on Saturday morning television. It is the first year they strongly identify with products sold through TV and therefore it's an active year for the "buy-me" syndrome. They also like Snoopy and all the Snoopy clothes, often preferring to play dress-up with Snoopy than with a doll. The small Mego super-hero dolls are popular (Spiderman, Batman, Wonder Woman, the Incredible Hulk), as are view-master sets. Trucks, tractors, wagons, and bikelike toys to drive or pull are good gifts.

Trips: Loves to go on a trip but has a rather short attention span. A trip or vacation with other children that involves doing something is advised. Likes to see and touch animals, do things with hands, and get involved. If he can't do it himself, or if it's too hard, he loses interest and becomes frustrated. May go hiking but will tire soon. Likes the beach, swimming pool, roller-skating, and activities with other children. Too young for long fishing trips, sightseeing, museums, or historical sights.

FIVE

General characteristics: A five cries often, may pick nose, bite fingernails, suck thumb. Likes to answer telephone and personify animals. Probably has favorite toy or "blanky." A five has a firm understanding of right and wrong. Wants to marry mother, father, or appropriate stepparent.

Appetite: May not eat good breakfast but should be interested in lunch and dinner. Does not like cooked vegetables. May begin to taste new foods. May want to eat what he has seen advertised on television.

Bathing and grooming habits: Cannot draw own bath, needs constant supervision, likes toys in bath.

Birthday festivities: Invite six children, lasts two to three hours, and requires constant entertainment—either movies or organized games. Each child likes to get a small gift or favor. Hats, noisemakers, and the usual accoutrements are a must.

Bladder control: May postpone going to bathroom, but show signs of needing to go—wiggling, hopping, grasping—without saying anything. Parents should learn the body language.

Books: Dragons Hate to be Discreet by Winifred Rosen, *Who Will Believe Tim Kitten?* by Jan Wahl, *Alexandra the Rock-Eater* by Dorothy Van Woerkom, *Clotilda* by Jack Kent.

Entertainment: Fives are quite grown-up in their demand for quality entertainment. They watch TV, want to see movies—particularly Walt Disney movies and stories about animals. They like to go to sports entertainment with adults, to watch parades, and go to plays.

Favorite color: One of the primaries.

Favorite holidays: Christmas and birthdays. Asks Santa for specific gifts. Wants to know all the details of Santa's life. May ask you to help write a letter to Santa. Also likes Halloween, Valentine's Day, Easter, and any other participatory holiday.

Food preferences: Cereals and candies advertised on Saturday morning television, hamburgers, spaghetti, fried chicken, chocolate pudding, sweets.

Gifts: Small cars and trucks, doctor/nurse kit, puppets or marionettes, Holly Hobby doll, Aggravation (Lakeside), Play Desk (Fisher Price), Super Socker Boppers (Skyline, Inc.).

Joke: Why did the little moron throw the clock out the window? He wanted to see time fly.

Motor capabilities: Walks up and down stairs the "grown-up" way, fastens buttons, laces shoes, ties bows, beginning to learn to roller skate, rides tricycle or hot wheels expertly, feeds self but cannot cut food.

Parental preference: Mother.

Peer play: Likes a lot of friends, sometimes prefers older children. Tends to be jealous easily.

Physical characteristics: Weight—40 pounds. Height —43 inches.

Responsibilities: Responsible enough to take care of pet with supervision from parents. Enjoys small responsibilities and jobs he can accomplish himself that make him feel grown-up.

School: Kindergarten. Very aware that next year he is starting school and sees that as an important growth stage.

Sexuality: Wants to know where babies come from. Very curious about pregnancy. Modest about his own body.

Skills: Can count to twenty, draw letters of alphabet, identify coins, knows name and address. Vocabulary up to two thousand words. Wants to learn to tell time. May be able to cross neighborhood streets by himself. Wants to learn to ride a two-wheeler.

Sleeping patterns: Wake-up—7:00–7:30 A.M. Bedtime—7:30–8:00 P.M. Nap—sometimes.

Television: Likes cartoon characters, superheroes and larger-than-life characters (the Incredible Hulk).

Toys and games: Dolls for boys and girls. Likes to play house, build with blocks, jump rope. Likes to play with pogo stick, on swings, and on jungle gyms. Often sex-role discrimination in games—boys play daddy, while girls play mommy.

Trips: Has a little more stamina and curiosity for family trips and vacations. Still needs to be active and be with other children but has more endurance and a longer interest span. May enjoy "exploring" but won't enjoy museums or historical sights. Take him anyplace he can be active and do something different—horseback riding, skating, swimming—and he will be happy, but don't be alarmed if he's afraid to try something new.

SIX

General characteristics: Very different from five-year-olds. Knows he is growing up. Proud to be losing teeth. May try to impress you with the fact he goes to school now and is no longer a baby. Complains about health—often to get attention. May cry easily. Likes his name on everything. Knows what is fantasy and what is reality.

Appetite: Strong all day long. Favors some foods to the exclusion of others. Probably doesn't like cooked vegetables. Notices if food is lumpy and may refuse to eat it.

Bathing and grooming habits: Baths are strongly resisted, especially by boys. Needs supervision and help in washing. May tell you he has washed when he hasn't. Needs to be reminded to wash face and hands after play and before meals.

Birthday: Birthdays are more important at six than at any previous age because the child is in school and he has all the excitement of peer participation. He usually wants two birthday parties, one at school and one on the weekend so his friends can come. Traditional parties are best with blowers, hats, cake and ice cream, games like Pin the Tail on the Donkey, etc. He may want to invite everyone in his class, which you don't have to accept.

Bladder control: May have occasional accident. Shy about telling teacher he has to go to bathroom.

Books: A Book of Elephants by Katie Wales, _Little Bear_ by Else Minarik, _Alexander Who Used to be Rich Last Summer_ by Judith Viorst, _Who's in Rabbit's House?_ by Verna Aardema.

Entertainment: Can begin to sit through a movie or follow a long television show.

Favorite color: Has one favorite color and wants everything to be that color.

Favorite holidays: Christmas, birthday, Valentine's Day, Easter, and after losing a tooth (believes in the tooth fairy). Likes Halloween if costume isn't scary.

Food preferences: Sugar-coated cereals, hamburgers, fried chicken, spaghetti, anything chocolate, peanut butter.

Gifts: Magic Set, Great Shapes, Junior Scrabble, Sorry, TV personality dolls, Clue, Operation (Milton Bradley).

Joke: Did all the animals on Noah's Ark come in pairs? No, the worms came in apples.

Motor capabilities: Likes to take things apart and try to put them back together, plays ball well, can dress and undress dolls, susceptible to falls, knows left from right.

Parental preference: Switching from mother to father.

Peer play: Plays well alone and with peers (in twosomes as general rule). Cliques may begin to form in schoo.

Physical characteristics: Weight—45 pounds. Height —46 inches.

Responsibilities: Six-year-olds were created to help out with family chores. They can do almost any simple task and do it well. Can feed pets (may need to be reminded), clear table, load dishwasher, help with the cooking, make bed, do laundry, etc. Sixes are usually anxious to help out, and with careful supervision make great elves!

School: First grade. He either loves or hates school. Tremendous authority given to teacher.

Sexuality: Wants to learn "dirty" words and giggles over anything that could be "dirty." Boys apt to expose themselves to girls. Knows difference between boys and girls. Wants to know how the baby gets out of mother's stomach during birth. Can grasp the baby-starts-from-seed concept.

Skills: Learning to read and print. May write letters backwards. Vocabulary improving daily.

Sleeping patterns: Wake-up—7:00–7:30 A.M. Bedtime—8:30–9:00 P.M. Sleeps with stuffed animal or live pet. Nap—rare.

Television: Favorite shows are "Brady Bunch," "Bewitched," "Mork and Mindy," "Osmond Family." Favorite personalities are Donny and Marie, Mork, or a superhero.

Toys and games: Hide-and-seek, tag, jump rope, roller skates, dolls, cowboys-and-Indians, cops-and-robbers. Begins to have interest in table games such as back-gammon, checkers, dominos, jigsaw puzzles. Likes to dress up in costume or adult clothes.

Trips: Visit to an amusement park or farm, fishing, camping, any activity that the family can do together.

SEVEN

General characteristics: More quiet than six, and appears more introverted and grown-up. Beginning to develop some independence in play. May be able to read well enough to entertain self. Eager to be friendly and win parental approval. Loves to give and get presents—no particular occasion is necessary.

Appetite: Moderate. Probably has extremes in eating—eats lots of his favorite foods and little of the ones he doesn't like. May try new tastes.

Bathing and grooming habits: Needs to be reminded to wash up. Supervision in shower or tub necessary. Less resistant to bathing than at six.

Birthday festivities: Trip to a theme park, activity with small group of friends, roller skating, movies, baseball game.

Books: Helga's Dowry by Tomi De Paola, *Carter Pig and the Ice Cream Lady* by Mary Rayner, *Caleb and Kate* by William Steig.

Entertainment: Can sit through a child-oriented movie, ballet or theater.

Favorite color: A primary.

Favorite holidays: Christmas and birthday. May know there isn't any Santa Claus, but doesn't care. Likes the tooth fairy and the Easter Bunny. Also likes Halloween and Valentine's Day.

Food preferences: Sugar-coated cereals, barbequed hot dogs, hamburgers, or chicken, steak and baked potatoes, french fries, fried chicken, junk food, sweets, ice cream, fruit-flavored yogurt, or frozen yogurt.

Gifts: Magic sets, jigsaw puzzles, celebrity dolls, models, items to start a collection (stamps, shells, etc.), subscription to a children's magazine or animal magazine.

Joke: What do you call a grocery clerk in China? A Chinese checker.

Motor capabilities: Can dress self, tie shoelaces, can't cut food, but uses eating utensils well.

Parental preference: Boys break away from their mothers.

Peer play: Plays well with others. May get loud and rambunctious within a group.

Physical characteristics: Weight—50 pounds. Height —48 inches.

Responsibilities: Sevens are anxious to help and when supervised can do a lot. They want to advance past the last year's simple tasks and may be overenthusiastic about how well they can do something. They should have regular chores that are theirs alone and may not need to be reminded—make bed, hang up clothes, etc. Always remind about pet care, just in case. Supervise more responsible tasks.

School: Second grade. Learning to write as well as print and may become avid reader. Vocabulary growing daily. Will try out new words on family. Will pick up slang expressions at school. Also imitates parents' speech patterns and expressions. Likes show-and-tell.

Sexuality: Very aware of differences between boys and girls. Shy about revealing his body to anyone, including parents. Very interested in how babies are born and grow in mother's stomach. May have boyfriend or girlfriend at school.

Skills: Can tell time. Girls want to learn to fix their own hair. Rides a two-wheeler now. Can count to one hundred and identify coins and bills. Plays with peers, does homework, reads. Girls may join Brownies or Bluebirds. Boys are eligible for Cub Scouts.

Sleeping patterns: Wake-up—7:00 A.M. Bedtime— 8:30–9:00 P.M. Nap—rare. Sleeps with favorite toy, stuffed animal or live pet.

Television: Favorite shows are "Mork and Mindy," "The Muppets," old reruns like "I Love Lucy." Favorite personalities are Mork and sports heroes.

Toys and games: Puzzles, board games, and do-it-yourself projects like paper dolls or chemistry sets, as well as crafts. Hopscotch, tag, hide-and-seek, make-believe.

Trips: Beach, amusement parks (especially Disneyland, Knotts Berry Farm, Magic Mountain). Not ready for sight-seeing at historical spots.

EIGHT

General characteristics: Eight has clearly made the transition from child to little adult. You will be amazed at how grown-up an eight-year-old is. Eights do everything fast—run around a lot using endless energy. Eights demand a lot of attention from parents. Telling tall tales is common. Very sensitive to criticism. Overly dramatic. May burst into tears for no reason or when overtired. Eights are usually very silly and enjoy making faces, giggling, and chanting nonsense rhymes. May begin talking on phone for entertainment. Very interested in collecting everything. Television is a strong influence as is television advertising. Hero worship of television and sports celebrities begins.

Appetite: Usually good. May smell food before eating. Not too willing to try new tastes.

Bathing and grooming habits: Resists bath. Can probably shower by himself. May need help washing hair and blowing it dry.

Birthday festivities: This is an age that likes to work off a lot of energy at parties so they should be planned accordingly. Recommended activities are ones that can burn off energy—roller-skating, ice-skating, swimming, or trampoline parties. Slumber parties may be requested but will be very noisy. There will invariably be someone who wants to go home in the middle of the night.

Books: *The Muppet Show Book* (pub. by Harry Abrams), *Tuckey the Hunter* by James Dickey, Nancy Drew/Hardy Boys series, *The Chronicles of Narnia* series, Star Trek/Star Wars/Galactica series, *The Witch of Blackbird Pond* by Elizabeth George Speare, *I Love My Mother* by Paul Zindel.

Entertainment: Likes the movies and may be able to sit through play if highly motivated. May begin to pressure parents for tickets to rock concerts. Likes to listen to radio and dance along.

Favorite color: Something exotic for girls (purple). A standard color for boys (brown or yellow).

Favorite holidays: His birthday, Christmas. Most eights know there is no Santa Claus or Easter Bunny. May want to stay up all night before Christmas to try to trap Santa.

Food preferences: Hamburgers, hot dogs, fried chicken, shrimp, lobster, steak, baked potatoes, corn on the cob, ice cream and cake, frozen- or fruit-flavored yogurt, apple pie, junk food, sweets, pizza.

Gifts: Magic set, celebrity doll, crafts sets, chemistry set, colored felt-tip pens, things to collect, kites, airplanes, car and plane models, skateboards, erector sets, dress-up clothes for girls.

Joke: What has a red nose and lives in a test tube? Bozo the Clone.

Motor capabilities: Ties shoes, cuts food somewhat but has difficulties with a knife. Learning to ride a two-wheeler. Advancing into athletic skills and learning to participate in adult sports. Handwriting is probably still too large and may be a bit wobbly.

Parental preference: Mother.

Peer play: Segregated play among children of the same age. Boys and girls may show some interest in each other. Pretty girls and handsome boys are identified as such. This is the first year of the "best friend" syndrome among children of same sex.

Physical characteristics: Weight—55 pounds. Height—50 inches.

Responsibilities: Not as eager to help out, but able to do jobs well. May try to fool you by cheating on chores and or saying that jobs were done when they weren't.

School: Third grade. Reading should be progressing to give child independence to read for enjoyment. May work with calculators and child-sized computers. Beginning to develop handwriting. No interest in history or the real world.

Sexuality: May not be clear on the facts of life. May just be learning about menstruation. Definitely picking up secondhand sexual information at school.

Skills: Should be able to tell time, draw in perspective, distinguish right from left. Handles knife and fork with some know-how. Should be able to ride bus and go on errands with older children. Can take airplane to visit another parent by self. Can answer telephone and take a simple message.

Sleeping patterns: Wake-up—7:00–7:30 A.M. Bed-time—8:30–9:00 P.M. Nap—rare.

Television: You can see the influence of television on your eight-year-old best by checking his handwriting and reading abilities. If his handwriting and reading are not up to par with your expectations (not his peers), you can see the extent of his television watching. There is a direct correlation between how sloppy the handwriting and how much TV is seen. Eight-year-olds have very adult viewing habits and will watch, or want to watch, almost anything offered, except documentaries and religious programs. They like high-action dramas with a super character (Wonder Woman, the Incredible Hulk) in which the normal person "saves the day." This coincides with their childhood fantasy of "saving the day" for adults. It is often possible to get an eight-year-old to read a book connected with a television show and thus use the electronic medium to boost the printed one. (There are also book versions of most children's movies.) Eight-year-olds should love to read—if they don't, they're watching too much television, and they love Mork.

Toys and games: Clue, Sorry, Parcheesi, backgammon.

Trips: A trip that involves physical participation—camping, horseback riding, riding the rapids. A theme park, only if you didn't go last year. Beginning to appreciate travel, but not much. Little interest in sight-seeing. May like to shop.

NINE

General characteristics: No longer childlike. Child is acquiring an air of independence, but particularly attached to home and family. Develops a passion for certain activities, foods, and people. Wants to be liked and thrives on praise. Able to do some activities on his own or with older children. "Can't wait" for upcoming events. Complains a lot. May feel terribly confused about stepparents due to enhanced loyalty to mother.

Appetite: Shows more adventure and flexibility but will get stuck on favorite foods—even if they are wildly exotic. Still turns down many new tastes.

Bathing and grooming habits: Will have to be coerced into bathing. May want supervision. Needs help washing hair.

Birthday festivities: A monster party with each guest dressed as his favorite monster. Screening of a "horror" movie.

Books: _Victorian Paper House_ by Evelyn Ness, _The Lemming Condition_ by Alan Arkin, _Abel's Island_ by William Steig, some serials and biographies.

Entertainment: Nines are getting sophisticated enough to make the move from children-oriented movies and theater into the real world. They still like movies about adventure, animals, and family struggles, but may like certain movie stars and want to see their work. They may also begin with the classics, like _Gone With the Wind._ They enjoy and appreciate musical theater, (although not serious dramatic theater), and probably want to go to concerts by rock stars. Nines may even be groupies.

Favorite color: Girls—exotic colors (turquoise or hot pink). Boys want something safe and male-oriented (navy blue, brown, or maybe dark green if it looks masculine).

Favorite holidays: Birthdays and Christmas. Halloween is a big favorite. Depending on how popular with peers, will like or dislike Valentine's Day. Knows the truth about Santa Claus but probably won't spoil it for younger siblings.

Food preferences: Has definite likes and dislikes. Usually prefers plain foods and old standards like hamburgers, roast beef, spaghetti, pizza, grilled cheese sandwiches.

Gifts: "English"-style bicycle, book backpack, Snoopy sleeping bag.

Joke: What's worse than raining cats and dogs? Hailing buses.

Motor capabilities: Can usually use knife and fork well and won't need help cutting food. Probably able to use blow dryer. Girls may be able to set hair in rollers.

Parental preference: Father for boys and mother for girls.

Peer play: May mingle with children of other sex but prefers to play with children of own sex. Clubs may be popular. Bullies, especially boys, are a problem in every group. If boys or girls have a "boyfriend" or "girlfriend," they will be shunned by peers. Usually has one best friend.

Physical characteristics: Weight—62 pounds. Height —52 inches.

Responsibilities: May want to know why he has to do so much work or gripe about his household duties, but is capable of many types of help—from making beds to cleaning of a more serious nature. Can cook and should be able to prepare a simple meal or help out with cooking when someone is sick. Can go to grocery store on errands, ride bus alone, carry own house key.

School: Fourth grade. Writes script rather than prints. Favorite subjects tend to fall into categories—math and science or history and art. Should be reading proficiently and is able to look up unfamiliar words in the dictionary. May be able to write songs or poetry and short stories. Natural abilities in arts and sciences are beginning to reveal themselves.

Sexuality: Understands menstruation and father's part in procreation. May say "dirty" words to get a reaction or tell smutty jokes. Girls closer to puberty than boys. "Early bloomers" may begin menses, development of breasts, pubic hair, etc.

Skills: Can do just about everything, though not proficiently. Handwriting is still difficult. Creative skills easily identified.

Sleeping patterns: Wake-up—7:00 A.M. Bedtime—9:00 P.M., but later on weekends. Nap—no. Nightmares are common.

Television: Favorite TV shows are "Happy Days," "Mork and Mindy," "Incredible Hulk," sporting events. Favorite TV heroes are Shaun Cassidy, Mork, and sports figures.

Toys and games: Nine-year-olds become choosy about their toys and games as their special interests begin to focus and talents emerge. "Girly" girls like dolls, while tomboy girls don't. Boys like models, racing sets, electronic toys and games. Girls may like do-it-yourself games or crafts kits. Old favorites like Monopoly, Clue, Scrabble, and so on are preferred when played with adults rather than peers.

Trips: Trip to exotic place. Wants to do something different and exciting, to have an adventure.

TEN

General Characteristics: Able to participate in adult conversations and voice own opinion. Shoulder shrugging is common. Girls' growth rate far ahead of boys. May begin talking about college, career, and marriage. Ready for sleepover camp. Adult behavior patterns begin to emerge.

Sense of humor is developing. Does not like adult interference. Being untidy is age-appropriate.

Appetite: More adventurous out of the regular home environment—may try new foods at a friend's house or in a restaurant. Picky about how he wants food made; might specify he wants it prepared "just like Mom makes it."

Bathing and grooming habits: Does not like to bathe or wash hair, though should be capable of accomplishing both alone. If left on his own, wouldn't bathe for a month.

Birthdays: Ten-year-olds are moving into more sophisticated parties—theme parties or trip parties with everyone going to a ballgame together or roller-skating. Perhaps children would like to come as their favorite Star Wars or Galactica figures. There may be boys and girls but expect them to keep to separate sides. A lot of rough play and rowdiness is to be expected.

Books: *Along Came the Model T* by Robert Quackenbush, *Beauty and the Beast* by Marianna Mayer, *Roll of Thunder, Hear My Cry* by Mildred Taylor, *The Upstairs Room* by Johanna Reiss, Nancy Drew series, Little House on the Prairie series.

Entertainment: Making the transition from kiddie movies to real feature films. A ten-year-old may enjoy a good science-fiction movie or maybe a musical. Old enough to sit through and enjoy a play. Girls may be well into ballet. Rock concerts and sporting events appreciated.

Favorite color: Girls are moving toward romantic colors (mauve or something equally soft). Boys like anything but pink (navy or dark green).

Favorite holidays: Birthday, Christmas, Valentine's Day, Halloween, St. Patrick's Day, Fourth of July.

Food preferences: Steak, hamburger, roast beef, French fries. Willing to try new foods, especially exotic ones like shrimp or lobster. Liver and asparagus are the most disliked foods. Decline in milk drinking may begin.

Gifts: Camera, Superfection (Lakeside), backgammon set, Nancy Drew or Hardy Boys mystery, Risk, fancy nightgown or brassiere for girls, teddy, advanced craft kits.

Joke: What New York building has the most stories? The public library.

Parental preference: The last year of hero worship. Boys and girls think that custodial parent is perfect.

Peer play: Sexes still mostly segregated. Competition between sexes is common with each feeling superior to the other. Development of team play and teamwork. Several "best friends" are common. Boys may tease girls, pull their hair, and push them around. Strong age for Brownies, Cub Scouts, etc.

Physical characteristics: Weight—67 pounds. Height —55 inches.

Responsibilities: Can make bed, clean room, take out trash, feed pets, do dishes, set table, cook simple meals.

School: Fifth grade. Interest in history and social studies developing. Should be proficient reader—reading at night with a flashlight is common at this age. Vocabulary consists of about fifty-five hundred words.

Sexuality: Knows more than you did at eighteen. More girls will be showing signs of puberty. No signs of puberty in boys.

Skills: Formal dance classes may begin, can cook a simple meal, may begin daytime baby-sitting jobs, can roller-skate, ice-skate, ride a two-wheeler bicycle. Learned artistic skills evolving. Music lessons appropriate.

Sleeping patterns: Wake-up—7:00 A.M. Bedtime—9:30 P.M. Nap—no.

Television: Television was probably made for ten-year-olds—they are at the height of their hero worship of TV characters and are most influenced by the language, fashions, and morals on the programs they watch. The action shows they prefer are moving away from the cartoon edge of "The Incredible Hulk" to the harder hitting police stories ("Vega$," "Charlie's Angels") with more action and more violence. They like fast cars, fight scenes, chases, and pretty girls. Boys also like to watch sports activities. May even pattern career goals after TV characters.

Toys and games: Ten-year-olds are moving away from toys and games and into their own special interests. This is a big age for collections, so ten-year-olds may well spend their time with coins, stamps, or historical treasures. Building models and kites is popular among boys (and should probably be encouraged in girls), dolls are still big sellers (celebrity and regular), stuffed animals are popular. Holly Hobbie is of interest to a lot of girls, and Snoopy remains popular with both sexes. Anything that has to do with science fiction ("Star Wars" and Buck Rogers, etc.) is popular.

Trips: Historical sites.

ELEVEN

General characteristics: Hates to help out. Very self-centered. Wants to see what he can get away with. Highly manipulative. Beginning of adolescence and the troublesome years parents don't expect until the child is thirteen. Eleven is sensitive, selfish, belligerent, defiant, jealous, argumentative, rude, uncooperative, and beginning the painful stage of passage from child to teeenager. Spends a lot of time deciding on what's fair and what's not, especially from parents. May want to move in with noncustodial parent while suffering from growing pains. May begin to experiment with smoking, drinking, drugs, and sex.

Appetite: Always thinking about eating. Boys eat

enormous amounts. Overweight children may be aware that they should diet.

Bathing and grooming habits: Less resistant to bathing, but may have to be prodded. Washing, drying, and styling hair may become a major preoccupation. Prefers shower to tub.

Birthday festivities: Should be very grown-up but not necessarily include both sexes. No babyish stuff here, though roller-skating and bowling parties are popular. Girls still like sleepovers. A grown-up celebration, going with the family and just one friend to a fancy restaurant and the theater, would be considered a treat.

Books: Bionic Parts for People by Gloria Skurzynski, *Dragonsinger* by Anne McCaffrey, *It's Not the End of the World* by Judy Blume, *Are You There, God? It's Me, Margret* by Judy Blume, the "Anne" series (*Anne of Green Gables,* etc.) by L. M. Montgomery.

Entertainment: Growing interest in movies, entertainment, and cultural events. Can now sit quietly through any performance—if he cares to! May want to see favorite movies over and over. Enjoys cultural activities with peers.

Favorite color: Blue for boys. Green, yellow, or turquoise for girls.

Favorite holidays: Birthday, Christmas, Valentine's Day.

Food preferences: Steak, roast beef, hamburgers, spaghetti, fried chicken, corn on the cob, soft drinks, diet drinks, cakes, fruit, candy, cookies, milk, junk food.

Gifts: Diary, pet (horse!), own telephone line, own television, clothes (particularly for girls), jigsaw puzzle.

Joke: What's a dead ringer? A deceased Avon lady.

Parental preference: Parents have lost their pedestal. Girls tend to prefer their fathers; they may do things to spite mother. Growing sexuality in girls will soon lead to flirting with fathers (and stepfathers).

Peer play: Has one "best" friend. Cliques strong. Boys and girls seldom play together. Might have crushes or even matched dates with friends of family. Doesn't make friends as easily as before. Fist fights and violent arguments are not uncommon. May belong to clubs, groups, or formal organizations. Goes ot overnight camp with a friend or group of friends. Likes to go to movies with peers rather than parents.

Physical characteristics: Weight—72 pounds. Height —57 inches.

Responsibilities: Can make bed, clean up room, hang up clothes, iron with supervision, cook, sew, hem, use washing machine, care for pets, help with younger children. Can do almost everything except drive. Capable ot taking good care of pets (may want larger, more expensive pets; this is the "horse crazy" stage).

School: Sixth grade. May be graduating from elementary school. Considers this a "passage." Should be able to read adult books and use growing vocabulary. After-school activities are important.

Sexuality: Breasts begin to develop and boys have erections. Many elevens are approaching puberty, most are beginning to get pubic hair. Peers may be in different stages of development. "Dirty" jokes are common at this age. Aware that they will marry yet shy of opposite sex. They understand menstruation, puberty, and reproductive system. Some girls will begin menses.

Skills: By this age they can learn anything they want. Sewing, auto repairs, carpentry, and advanced crafts' skills can all be mastered. Determination to learn the new skill is an important factor. May need supervision while in the learning stages.

Sleeping patterns: Wake-up—7:30–8:00 A.M. (sleeps later on weekends). Bedtime—10:00–11:00 P.M. (later on weekends). Nap—no.

Television: Favorite programs are sports, "Happy Days," "Laverne and Shirley," "Charlie's Angels." Favorite TV personalities are one of Charlie's Angels, a rock idol or a leading sports figure.

Toys and games: Elevens are so grown-up play items can no longer be supplied through toy shops. They have their own special interests—in crafts, reading, and hobbies that need to be catered to. By age eleven, definite talents exist and need to be practiced or further developed. Elevens do roller-skate, ride bikes, play backgammon and card games, skateboard, participate in team sports, refinish furniture, paint, take dance lessons, play with doll houses, and talk on the phone.

Trips: Historical sites and "adult" vacations to new places are now of interest. Still interested in theme parks but may consider them boring if you went there in the past. Because elevens are more peer than family oriented, a good vacation is one where he can be with friends his own age.

TWELVE

General characteristics: Very interested in everything and approaches all activities with enthusiasm. Very competitive. They appear to be maturing so you're always surprised when they do something childish. Don't need a baby-sitter. They like "hanging around," don't want parental direction. Both sexes conscious of appearances. Girls may be "primping." May have questions about your divorce and remarriage. They feel loyal to custodial parent, but are confused about what happened to their parents' marriage.

May be very angry if a divorce or remarriage takes place while at this age.

Appetite: Insatiable. Eats big meals and snacks. May fill up on junk food. May give new foods a try.

Bathing and grooming habits: Actually realizes they *need* to bathe. Boys and girls seem to prefer simplicity of showers. Girls may need help blow-drying hair, but should manage by themselves. Fingernails may need checking. Both sexes take a sudden interest in their personal appearance. Interested in the appearance of their room and their home. May even volunteer to clean up or redecorate.

Birthday festivities: A slumber party, a dance for boys and girls (make sure everyone gets to dance), a special activity for a small group of three or four (dinner and a play).

Books: Twelve-year-olds are so grown up they often read adult-level books, best sellers, books of special interest, or young-adult novels, which are sold in a special section of most book stores. They like all "Judy Blume" books, *Phoebe* by Patricia Diznzo, *Diary of a Frantic Kid Sister* by Hila Colman, *Me, Mom and Wolfman* by Norma Klein, *Seventh Summer* by Maureen Daly. Warning—most young-adult books are written for girls (all of the above are) and often deal with sex, unwanted pregnancy, first love, rape, abortion, and remarriage. Know your authors, or what you are buying!

Entertainment: Likes to go out with peers or "gangs" rather than family to concerts, movies, roller-skating rinks, bowling alleys, or dances.

Favorite color: Girls will be very influenced by fashion colors. Their favorite colors will be those that are most popular in fashion and magazines and colors that show some sophistication. Boys like brown.

Favorite holidays: Birthday, Christmas, Valentine's Day.

Food preferences: Steak and potatoes, McDonald's, fast food.

Gifts: Diary (for girls), tickets to a rock concert, record albums, stereo, clothes, hair dryer, gymnastics lessons, camera.

Joke: Probably likes "dirty" jokes. Also enjoys puns, jokes, gags, and other people with a sense of humor. Sense of humor is developed almost to capacity.

Parental preference: Father (mom is too strict.)

Peer play: Peer pressure is extreme. Definite interest in boys and girls as "boyfriends" and "girfriends," although crushes are generally short-lived. Parties and school activities almost always include both sexes. "Best friend" syndrome is still common. Plays with older children and may have role model a few years older.

Physical characteristics: Weight—77 pounds. Height —60 inches.

Responsibilities: Twelves can cook, clean house, wash cars, and do anything but drive. Can take on small jobs for money like babysitting, paper route, lawn mowing, etc. State laws prohibit full-time employment until the age of sixteen.

School: Seventh grade. Thinks they are very grown up and that grade school was easy. May say they dread the harder subjects of junior and senior high, but is really looking forward to them. School cliques have already developed and a child's position in the clique is defined and will probably remain stable. Cheating may be common to their clique in school and accepted morally.

Sexuality: Many girls are menstruating, have breasts, and pubic hair. Shy about changes in body. Girls maturing much more rapidly than boys. Pubic hair developing in boys. Increased growth in penis and scrotum. Erections and nocturnal emissions occur often. Both sexes are interested in sex and are quite aware of their growing sexuality. Any word with a possible double meaning makes them giggle.

Skills: Can learn almost anything and perfect skills with practice. Sports and musical skills can be spotted. Natural talents probably will have appeared before age twelve, but can be developed more each year. By age twelve, child is ready to get serious about potential of his talent. Writing ability has been slowly developing since age ten and is now a new tool of communication—plays, poems, stories, and songs pour out. May have foreign pen pals. For the first time letter writing is easy.

Sleeping patterns: Wake-up—7:30–8:00 A.M. Bedtime—10:00–11:00 P.M. Nap—no.

Television: Prefers action shows and TV movies, sporting events and favorite reruns. TV habits are already developed and broken only by disciplinary measures. May like documentaries about animals.

Toys and games: Twelve-year-olds are part child and part adult, so their toys and games are a combination of both. Active in team sports, usually take lessons to develop talent, play backgammon and card games, and prefer to hang out with adults rather than play with younger children when given the opportunity. They still play board games, read, bike, and skate as well as follow special interests and hobbies. Twelves may have a serious hobby that takes up their free time, a horse to ride and care for, a doll house to refurbish, a baseball team to play on, etc. Good books are the best game to keep on hand for twelve-year-olds.

Trips: An adult-oriented vacation. Now old enough to sightsee. May want to go to Europe or travel with a school group to different parts of the country or world. Prefers a vacation with peers, not family.

10.
Don't Call
Me Mommy
Unless Your
Mother Approves

I just love movies about cowboys and Indians, wagon trains, and pioneers. So when some soppy saga of the West came on the Saturday night movie recently, Mike moved to the living room to listen to some records and I happily stayed in bed watching the show. It began with a wedding and a pioneer daddy taking a walk for the old heart-to-heart talk with his sixteen-year-old son.

Pioneer Man: "Boy, I know you don't take kindly to my marrin' again, but Jessie's a real fine woman. I love her and I need her. She'll be a good mom to you kids. Give her a chance, boy."

Boy and his young sister had, of course, no such intention. Jessie, it turned out, who was as pretty, delicate, friendly, and sincere as one must be to get this kind of part, was the perfect stepmother. By day she drove the wagon until her hands were raw, while by night she cooked gourmet campfire dinners. Then, when the whole family had gone to bed, she sat up by candlelight to make little treats for the kids. When the little girl lost her rag doll, Jessie worked all night making a new doll. Her only thanks: "My real mommy would have done it better."

Twenty minutes into the show, before the Indians attacked and the little girl got lost in the woods, I was in tears. In tears for Jessie and myself, for Amy, and for all the stepparents who have shared the final insult and smiled through gritted teeth. "My real mommy would have done it better. You're not my real mommy."

I became a stepparent feeling much like Jessie did, trying to do my best and anxious to please. Maybe too anxious. It's hard to remember. I pursued my idealistic and romantic dreams of who and what I was to this child until harsh reality allowed me no further illusions. Despite the fact that I made her meals, defended her from bumblebees, and braided her hair each morning, she was unable to allow me entry into her life. Whereas at the end of the movie and one-half box of Kleenex later, the pioneer family had beaten off the Indians, found the lost little girl, and realized what a wonderful woman Jessie was, I could not find the same happy ending.

At first, I liked being a stepmother. In fact, I *loved* being a stepmother. In my case, because the child was living with us for a longer period of time, I was a mother and saw myself that way. I was a part-time full-time mother, and I liked it. In return, I found a child anxious to please me, wanting to be loved. She was easy enough to accept into my life and enough like me as a child that I often was able to believe she was my own child. She called me Mommy; I called her my daughter. I thought the drastic changes in my life since her arrival were part of motherhood. I thought it was my problem to adjust. I was pleased to see I was a good mother. I hadn't had much training for the job and most people in my family thought I would have a difficult time transforming myself from the *Cosmo* girl into the *Redbook* mother.

It was all so new and exciting to me that when things started to go wrong, I didn't know enough to see what was happening. I thought that must be how things are; I thought I needed to adjust better. If I resented that we no longer had time, energy or privacy for sex, I berated myself for not knowing that was how it was with parents. (After all, as a teenager I was convinced that my parents never "DID IT.") If I had no time for make-up, solitary bubble baths, and novels about women in pretty dresses, I remembered that my mother never wore make-up, took showers at 6:30 in the morning before she cooked breakfast for the family, and never read a trashy book in her life. If I hated my husband's first wife, I chided myself for being uncivilized. She is a charming woman with whom I wanted to be friendly and I was determined to overcome the pettiness surrounding the usual wife/ex-wife relationships. I would learn to love my husband's first wife.

No one ever sat me down and told me that I came first. No one ever told me it was healthy to hate my husband's first wife and that I should never have to speak to her in my life if I didn't want to. I didn't know how to stop playing the sophisticate, "Oh, yes, we're all one big happy family," to do a little bit of my own yelling to get a little bit of what I wanted. No one ever told me that the marriage I was trying desperately to make perfect was headed for destruction if I were unable to open my own mouth and say what I felt, what I wanted and what I needed to make me happy. I didn't even guess that a child was capable of breaking up a marriage. My marriage.

After two years of stepmotherhood, I had memories of long walks on the beach collecting seashells with my daughter; the time I wore her bathing suit because my own got eaten by a dog, and the day she lost her baby blanket and was grown-up enough to bypass tears. I also had an ulcer. I had a ribbon of resentment growing throughout my being. It went back as far as the day Amy arrived and I hadn't been allowed to meet her at the plane and continued through the days I had been forced to take her to work with me. In my earnest endeavor to be perfect I forgot that no one was ever perfect. In my attempts to do the right thing and be the mother my mother was, I lost my sense of my own self.

While I desperately love the little girl in my life, I was seething with anger, hurt and confusion. There was no room for me at her birthday party. The school was embarrassed when I cooked for the bake sale. The children in the car pool could not remember my name. My weekends were being lost to a child who never even said thank you and who occasionally wrote me hate letters.

The problem was mine. I had not read the fine print in the contract. I did not know the difference between being a parent and being a stepparent. I did not know that perseverance would *not* pay off. I had dedicated myself to the one day I would overhear Amy telling a friend, "My stepmother was really terrific to me. You wouldn't believe all the neat things we did when I was growing up because she cared about me so much."

Alas, the sentence I had been dreaming of was a bit of a run-on and not even fitted to Amy's speech pattern. She would never say that. It was better to admit it now and live through my disappointment. It was better to think of myself first . . . and my husband and my marriage. It was better to fight for me and for Mike. And that was how I discovered exactly what is required for a stepparent to live happily ever after.